Index Press

FAR FROM THE MASTERS

EXPERIMENTATIONS IN POST-NEW WAVE FRENCH CINEMA

Edited by
Conall Cash and Corey P. Cribb

Far from the Masters:
Experimentations in Post-New Wave French Cinema

Series: Experimental Cinemas

First published in Australia in 2025 by Index Press
Printed in Australia

Index Press
The Nicholas Building
Suite 703, 37 Swanston Street
Naarm Melbourne VIC 3000
Australia

index-press.com

Index Press acknowledges and pays respect to the elders of the Kulin Nations as the owners of the lands and waters on which we live and work. Aboriginal sovereignty was never ceded.

Index Press Inc. is an incorporated association registered in Victoria, Australia

Series Editor: Giles Fielke
Proofreading: Sam Cooney
Design: Yanni Florence

ISBN: 978-0-64862-974-0

A catalogue record for this book is available from the National Library of Australia.

CONTENTS

Introduction
Conall Cash and Corey P. Cribb 1

Square One: *Le Pont du Nord* (1981)
Jake Wilson 11

No Messing with Love: *À nos amours* (1983)
Conall Cash 21

Epigones and Enfants: *L'Amour fou* (1969)
Miranda Stanyon 31

An Ode to Headlessness: *Acéphale* (1968)
Corey P. Cribb 45

Salvation and Civilisation: *L'Enfant sauvage* (1970)
Jack Keenan 53

Anybody Can Be Somebody: *Les Idoles* (1968)
Philippa Hawker 69

Tourists of a Sentimental History: *Visages Villages* (2017)
Scott Robinson 87

202 Minutes at The Capitol: *Jeanne Dielman, 23 Quai du Commerce, 1080 Bruxelles* (1975)
Michelle Huang 101

Index of Films Cited 109

Acknowledgments 112

Conall Cash and Corey P. Cribb

Introduction

The essays collected in this book emerged from a film club devoted to French cinema, held at the University of Melbourne from 2022 to 2023. The idea of the film club was simple enough: to use our positions at the university to create a space for watching and discussing films. We invited scholars, critics, filmmakers, and students to select films and introduce screenings. As the club developed and the network of participants grew, a more specific focus emerged: a shared fascination with the diverse strands of French cinema that emerged after the mid-1960s, when the energies of the New Wave (or *nouvelle vague*) began to splinter in new directions. A symposium, "After the New Wave: Cinema, History, Belatedness," took place in March 2023, developing these concerns with longer research presentations. This book is, in part, the story of a small group of cinephiles discovering and cultivating a shared interest in a relatively neglected group of films made on the other side of the world: the story of a film club as a meeting place. "Cinema," as Jean-Luc Godard once memorably remarked, is "the goodwill for a meeting," and the French cinema which emerged from, parted ways with, and reflected upon the *nouvelle vague* became the occasion for this meeting of ours.[1]

In retrospect, it seems we were on to something. Not long after we started on this focus, post-New Wave French cinema

1 Jean-Luc Godard, "The Carrots Are Cooked: A Conversation with Jean-Luc Godard," interview by Gideon Bachmann. *Film Quarterly* 37, no. 3 (Spring 1984): 16.

took on something of a wider renaissance. Near the end of 2022, the *Sight and Sound* Critics Poll declared an unexpected new entry in the position of "greatest film of all time": Chantal Akerman's *Jeanne Dielman, 23 Quai du Commerce, 1080 Bruxelles* (1975), a key work of post-New Wave cinema (Belgian, not French, to be sure, but made by a filmmaker raised on, and remaining in close connection with, French cinema). Then, months after our grainy screenings to a small group of dedicated viewers of two epic works of this same post-New Wave moment—Jacques Rivette's *L'Amour fou* (1969) and Jean Eustache's *La Maman et la putain* (*The Mother and the Whore*, 1973)—it was announced that these same two films would be restored and re-released. Something about post-New Wave French cinema was provoking new interest around the world, and our small group found itself a part of this moment.

As different as the three films mentioned above are, together they indicate many of the shared ambitions and preoccupations of post-New Wave cinema. In many films of this post-New Wave moment, we find a turn away from the innocence or lightness of discovery and invention prevalent in the films of the New Wave, and in its place a certain heaviness, felt as much in the formal asceticism of these films as in their often-sombre themes. This heaviness, as the essays in this collection show, expresses a renewed concern for the weight of both social and cinematic history, a meditation on what it means to inherit, to arrive *after*. At the same time, films like the three just mentioned (two of which receive more extensive readings in the essays that follow) renew the New Wave's principle of a commitment to the singularity of an artistic vision, irrespective of professional experience or budgetary constraints.

What we call the *experimentation* of post-New Wave cinema involves this combination of a rigorous commitment to artistic creation and a critical, self-conscious reckoning with the cinematic image and its histories. Post-New Wave experimentations work to renew the creative powers of cinema in and through their critical inheritance of film and media history. This, we suggest, is what makes this moment in French cinema ripe for contemporary rediscovery and engagement. As the ubiquity of screen images in our own media landscape tends to flatten historical consciousness, post-New Wave experimentation offers another model of image production, in which a critical inheritance of the history of images informs the work of creation itself. With regard to the three films named above, we might mention *L'Amour fou*'s play with documentary and fiction, *Jeanne Dielman*'s problematisation of received images of women in cinema, and *La Maman et la putain*'s concern with truth attained through formal minimalism as instances of this simultaneously critical and experimental spirit of post-New Wave cinema.

***

The term "post-New Wave" evokes an attitude or outlook as much as a chronologically defined period. Given that the historical contours of the New Wave itself are already infamously difficult to define (with the debate ongoing as to whether Agnès Varda's 1955 *La Pointe Courte* or Claude Chabrol's 1958 *Le Beau Serge* should be recognised as the first genuine *nouvelle vague* film), the *post* in post-New Wave comes with its own dose of indeterminacy, implying at once an affinity with its precursor and a desire to overcome or transcend the New Wave's limits. Whereas the alternative term "late New Wave" suggests continuity, the idea of the "post-New Wave" carries with it the ambivalent sense of both a break and an inheritance. If the New Wave stood for a revolutionary, energetic reinvention of cinema, what does it mean to come *after* that moment has passed? This difficult inheritance found responses from the new generation of directors—including Akerman, Eustache, Marguerite Duras, Philippe Garrel, and Maurice Pialat—that ranged from melancholy and nostalgia to irony and violent refutation.

Of course, there was a larger revolutionary event or process that would leave its mark on post-New Wave cinema in France, in the political struggles that reached their crescendo in May 1968. May '68 posed the question of what an anti-capitalist revolution could look like in a hyper-mediated consumer society, leading to an interrogation of the politics of the image which would inform the radical cinema of the period. Famous slogans of the movement such as "Sous les pavés, la plage" ("Under the paving-stones, the beach") involved a call to overcome the distracted, passive state of capitalist life (a world described by Guy Debord as a "society of the spectacle"), so as to rediscover a realm of freedom and possibility by looking differently at the present.[2] While not all post-New Wave filmmakers were supporters of '68 and its vision of emancipatory politics, there is a palpable sense that *after* '68 one had to make films differently than before. On the more politically radical end stands Godard, a founding New Wave figure who became one of its sharpest critics in the post-New Wave moment. In a programmatic statement of the goals of his short-lived collaboration with Jean-Pierre Gorin as the Dziga Vertov Group, Godard declares his intention to "make films politically" rather than merely "mak[ing] political films"—a key expression of this new politicisation of the process of making and projecting cinematic images.[3] Varda's films of this period, in their interrogation of the cinematic construction of gender,

2 Guy Debord, *The Society of the Spectacle*, trans. Ken Knabb (Critical Editions, 2021). Originally published as *La Societé du spectacle* (Buchet-Chastel, 1967).

3 Jean-Luc Godard, "What is to be done?", trans. Mo Teitelbaum, in *The Afterimage Reader*, ed. Mark Webber (The Visible Press, 2022), 37. Originally published in *Afterimage* no. 1 (April 1970).

participate in this same political self-reflection upon image production that became especially prominent in the post-'68 moment.[4] Filmmakers like Garrel and Eustache, meanwhile, each took up in their own way this post-'68 suspicion towards cinematic spectacle, seeking to return cinema to its original promise, which had been forgotten by the prevailing regime of the image.

***

But a cinema that interrogates and even turns against the image cannot easily be a happy one, even if its ambitions are revolutionary. How is cinema to go on after the naïve belief in cinema's innocence has been destroyed? How does one go on making films after one has been awakened to cinema's role in serving a politics of mass distraction and pacification? A new tone of harshness enters the scene in this period, with Godard's 1966 film *Masculin féminin* providing perhaps its first expression, anticipating the larger transformation that would occur after '68. Godard's film—which shocked many, including his old friend François Truffaut—depicts a mutual incomprehension, if not contempt, between men and women of the new generation, seeming to drain all the life out of the New Wave, with its romanticisation of youth, the city, and the inventive powers of cinema. Opening up (or perhaps renewing) a deeply anti-romantic strain in French cinema, *Masculin féminin* may be the first film to both announce and reflect on the death of the New Wave, and the dreams it stood for.

Amidst the brutality, one scene stands out for its melancholy: a scene which, fittingly enough, takes place at a cinema. Jean-Pierre Léaud, as Paul, narrates his and others'

4 See Varda's comments in "The Pleasures of Existence," interview by Aline Desjardins, trans. Conall Cash, *e-flux* (July 2025).

disappointment at the films they now find themselves watching. Paul, in words liberally adapted (without acknowledgement) from Georges Perec's 1963 novel *Things*, gives expression in voiceover to the unity of cinema and life that the New Wave had seemed to offer, as well as to the disappointment and difficulty of living in the aftermath of its failure:

> We were disappointed. The dated images flickered on the screen, and Marilyn Monroe had aged terribly. We were sad. This wasn't the film we had dreamed of. This wasn't that total film which each one among us carried in themselves. That film we had wanted to make, or, more secretly, that we had wanted to live.[5]

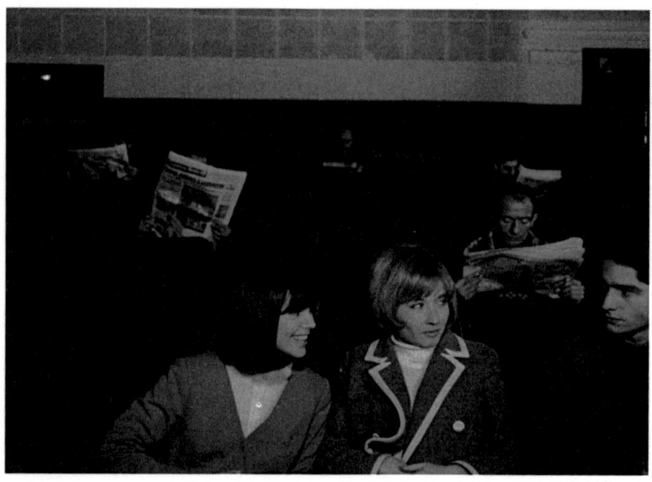

This dream of the total film, of life lived as if it were as ceaselessly vibrant and interconnected as a film—the

5 Cf. Georges Perec, *Things: A Story of the Sixties*, trans. Andrew Leak (Harper Collins, 1991), 57.

dreamworld of Jules and Jim running on the bridge with Jeanne Moreau, in Truffaut's 1961 film—seems to have died by this moment, and Godard now assigns himself the task of performing its autopsy. Adding insult to injury for Truffaut, Godard casts Léaud—whose legendary appearance in Truffaut's *Les Quatre Cents Coups* (*The 400 Blows*, 1959) at the tender age of fourteen marked a foundational moment of the New Wave—as this alternately melancholic and embittered harbinger of the movement's impending end.

Seven years later, Léaud again, in his role as Alexandre in *La Maman et la putain*, offers a still harsher expression of this sense of having missed the moment, and of seeing the dreams of a reintegrated life dissolve into a set of images. "I'm certain," Alexandre complains,

> that everything that's happened in the world in recent years is totally directed against me. There was the Cultural Revolution, May '68, the Rolling Stones, long hair, the Black Panthers, the Palestinians, the Underground—and now for the past two or three years, nothing.

By 1973, we have moved from Godard/Perec's mourning of the dream of a "total film" to Eustache's miserable individual who feels the world is "totally directed against" him, because he has missed the great political events and countercultural moments of the late '60s, and now feels himself stuck in the "nothing" of what comes after. If the post-New Wave period began around '68, with the hope of linking a cinematic critique of image-production to a social movement for radical change and democratisation, a few years later it might be said that the critique found itself without a movement. In such a moment, personal disaffection, and the sense that images could no longer do the work of binding individuals to collective meanings, struggles, or dreams, became increasingly prominent.

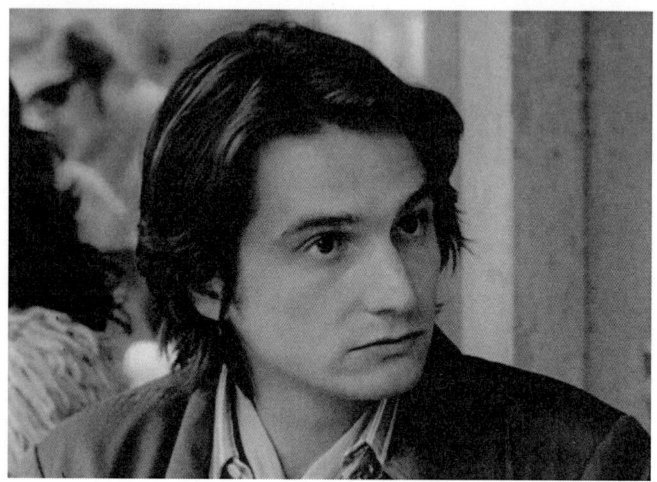

This renewed attention to the personal, and to the breakdown of a meaningful connection between personal and collective life that was once encapsulated in that dream of the "total film," will be one recurring quality of post-New Wave films, in their ambivalent inheritance of the cinema and the politics of the sixties. The three films we began this introduction with—*La Maman et la putain*, *Jeanne Dielman*, and *L'Amour fou*—are exemplary of this tendency of the post-New Wave moment towards a crisis in the relation between personal life and collective meaning, and a sense that the time of their union has passed. Eustache's film will occupy this space of personal frustration and belatedness across its four-hour run-time, revealing a nasty underside to the utopian dream of seeking to live the revolution. Here, in the absence of the collective movements Alexandre has missed, revolution can be made only in personal life—something that for him mostly takes the form of petty, misogynistic outbursts. Akerman's *Jeanne Dielman* famously looks in painstaking detail at the everyday actions of its titular character, a widow upholding the duties of a homemaker with striking, obsessive precision. Rivette's *L'Amour fou* shows the deterioration of a relationship into madness and retreat from the world. The extended length of these films serves only to underscore the loss of any link between personal life and collective action, as the films sink deeper and deeper into a world of private obsessions and rituals.

***

Something else happened during the run of our film club, which marked another end of the French New Wave, and another moment for reflecting on what it means to come after it: in September 2022, Godard died. We responded by going to the movies. On the night following the announcement of Godard's death, several of us involved in the film club attended a screening of independent Melbourne filmmaker Ivan Gaal's work at the "Unknown Pleasures" series at the Thornbury Picture House. Afterwards, three of us were on a tram home going down High Street, trading ideas about the evolution of Gaal's work as we'd been presented it in that evening's showcase. It was after 11 pm on a Tuesday, and the tram was nearly empty, but we remained standing, for there was too much to talk through and no time to think of taking a seat. We avoided mentioning Godard, whose loss hung over things that night—but something of his enthusiasm was felt, as we took up the work of continuing to think and talk about images.[6]

It's a statement of Godard's that provides the title of this book. In his film *Scénario de Sauve qui peut (la vie)* (1979),[7] Godard

6 We learnt of Gaal's own death, three years later in September 2025, just prior to the completion of this book.

7 This film was Godard's submission to the Centre national du cinéma in search of funding for his film *Sauve qui peut (la vie)*, which was subsequently made and released the following year.

addresses the audience from his editing suite, inviting us into the collaborative work of interrogating his own production of images. "Nous sommes dans la cuisine," he says, referring to the editing suite, "loin des maîtres. Et ça c'est déjà quelque chose." ("We're in the kitchen, far from the masters. And that's already something.") Being in Australia can also feel like being in the back room, out of sight—especially for those Australians who like to fill their heads with French movies. So it is good to be reminded that it's often in those ignored spaces that the real creative work—the work of making and unmaking images—gets done. The essays in this volume all respond to the creative and critical potential opened up by post-New Wave French cinema, from the perspectives of antipodean writers, scholars, and filmmakers, writing far from many of our own masters, including Godard himself.[8] The collection doesn't aim to be exhaustive of this vast field of French cinema, nor are we all scholarly experts in the directors or periods our essays focus on; what the essays prioritise is the experience of an encounter with a single film, and the creative work of investigation that this encounter gives rise to. In the kitchen, the workshop, or in the lecture theatre that became our screening room—to write and think with images in the spirit of post-New Wave cinema is to find oneself, and one's thinking, far from the masters.

8 All of the essays respond to films made between 1968 and 1983, with the exception of Scott Robinson's essay on Agnès Varda and JR's *Visages Villages* (2017)—a film which, as Robinson explores, is defined by its mixed inheritance of the *nouvelle vague*.

Jake Wilson

Square One: *Le Pont du Nord* (1981)

Let's go back to starting positions. It's really much more comfortable.

Dale Cooper's Doppelgänger in *Twin Peaks: The Return* (David Lynch, 2017)

1

In the films of Jacques Rivette, there's always the question of a *return to origins*: the origin of cinema in his earliest silent shorts, or the origin of Western drama in the tragedies rehearsed by the characters in his epic serial *Out 1* (1971). The theatrical exercises that dominate the first ninety-minute episode of *Out 1* suggest a more primordial kind of beginning: deprived of both language and mobility, the actors thrash around on the floor like infants, or prehistoric creatures who have only recently made it onto dry land.[1]

A decade on, *Le Pont du Nord* marked a new beginning for Rivette himself: his first completed film in several years, following a reported nervous breakdown and the collapse of his ambitious four-film project *Scènes de la vie parallèle*. At this moment—the end of the 1970s—it could also be said that the notion of having to rebuild from scratch was in the air more generally, especially among artistic and political

1 The texts by Jacques Rivette and Serge Daney cited in this piece are reprinted in the booklet accompanying the 2013 Masters of Cinema DVD of *Le Pont du Nord*, translated into English by Craig Keller, who is also the booklet's editor.

radicals forced to come to terms with the fading of utopian dreams. Reviewing *Le Pont du Nord* in the newly launched daily *Libération*, the critic Serge Daney hinted as much, describing Rivette and his onetime comrades of the *nouvelle vague* as "starting once again from square one from this fictive and documentary Paris which was the scene of their debuts."[2]

"Most of the time, it started like this," reads the title card that opens Rivette's *Céline et Julie vont en bateau* (*Celine and Julie Go Boating*, 1974), suggesting that the series of events we are about to witness is just one iteration of an endless cycle. As this implies, the ritual gesture of wiping the slate clean can be seen, paradoxically, as a matter of business as usual—and as an alibi for the repetition of the same motifs and devices encountered the last time round. "Starting over," in other words, is an oxymoron, entailing a continued relation to the past nominally set aside. Whatever journey we embark on, among our companions there are always ghosts.

2

Ghosts of the future, even. Before anything else, *Le Pont du Nord* endures as a precious record of the acting gifts of Pascale Ogier, who died of a heart attack in 1984 at the age of 25. For a viewer with prior knowledge of this, the most jarring moment in the film comes early on: Ogier's character, Baptiste, is riding her motorcycle down a Parisian alley, when she swerves to avoid an older woman with her head in a book. Following an offscreen crash, we dwell on the horrified response of Marie, the woman in question—played by none other than *nouvelle vague* icon Bulle Ogier, Pascale's mother. Then we cut to Baptiste on

2 Serge Daney, "On *Le Pont du Nord*,", trans. Craig Keller. In *Le Pont du Nord* DVD booklet (Masters of Cinema, 2013): 27. Originally published in *Libération*, March 26th, 1982.

the ground, lying with her head beneath a parked car; after a moment she climbs to her feet, seemingly unharmed.

These characters are strangers to one another, but the film will be a chronicle of the alliance that springs up between them, as well as a documentary on this actual parent and child acting side by side. Still more than the heroines of *Céline et Julie*, Marie and Baptiste make a classically contrasted pair: fair and dark, gun moll and space cadet, feet-on-the-ground and head-in-the-clouds. As Daney noted, the contrast is also a "description of two generations," a conception that brings its own set of paradoxes.[3] Newly back on the streets after a stint in prison, Marie is a tough cookie on the outside—yet she remains something of a hippie at heart, retaining her belief in love, in existential freedom, even in the political ideals that propelled her towards a life of crime.

Both more innocent and more disillusioned, Baptiste is a fatalist with a gnostic streak, viewing her environment in the Manichean terms of pure paranoia. Scowling in her leather jacket, she disavows any specific backstory: she's a warrior from Elsewhere, the way Clint Eastwood was the Man With No Name. At the same time, there's a comic side to her alienation, her stern pale face evoking the tradition of the "white clown"—perhaps the source of her chosen alias, shared with Jean-Louis Barrault's character in *Les Enfants du Paradis* (Marcel Carné, 1945). Her kung-fu poses imply both a reverence for tradition and a modern willingness to borrow moves from anywhere; her chunky white headphones set her at a distance from her surroundings, anticipating cyberpunk fiction and the subsequent rise of the internet, a fenced-off playground where many kinds of new connections become possible. She may be off on her own planet, but she's *wired in.*

3 Daney, "On *Le Pont du Nord*," 26.

3

"This isn't a game": Baptiste repeats this refrain every chance she gets. But she may be protesting too much: like every Rivette film, *Le Pont du Nord* can be understood as a game with definite rules, although one such rule is that the rules themselves can shift. Another rule in this instance is that everything has to happen *en plein air*, no interiors allowed. The justification for this prohibition varies, depending on whose angle you see it from: for Rivette, it might be firstly a budget thing, for Marie, it's claustrophobia exacerbated by her jail time, while for Baptiste, it's a means of staying off the grid (though her strategy wouldn't achieve much in contemporary Paris, or most big cities of the twenty-first century, when ubiquitous surveillance is too taken for granted to merit reflection, let alone resistance). From time to time, the rule is bent or broken: Marie and Baptiste briefly venture onto the elevated metro and snatch a few hours' sleep in an all-night movie theatre. But Rivette's camera doesn't accompany them on the latter occasion, when there may in any case be a technical loophole: the film screening is *The Big Country* (William Wyler, 1958), the French title of which, *Les Grands Espaces*, could be translated back into English as *The Great Outdoors*.

Further rules are more esoteric. After Baptiste pilfers a sheaf of documents from Marie's lover, Julien, the two women find themselves playing a game, with the city as the board—specifically, the Game of the Goose, a Snakes and Ladders prototype popular in Europe since the seventeenth century. Etymologically, there may be no link with the English phrase "wild-goose chase," but this could nonetheless describe their trajectory as they spiral from the heart of the city to its outskirts, following a trail whose waystations include a series of parks, squares, underpasses, vacant blocks, and construction sites: places that belong to everyone and no one, havens for the idle and for those with nowhere to go. Another return to beginnings, to a game for children which is also the primal game of cinema: starting from the accessible surface and seeking to uncover or imagine what lies beneath, which might be termed the occult world or the world of grown-ups.

4

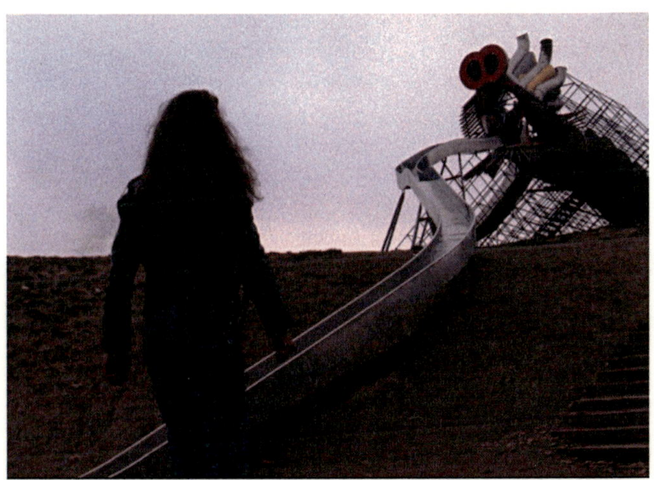

Yet another frequent rule for Rivette is to start from a literary text, or several such texts, which need not mean that the finished work qualifies as anything like a direct adaptation. In *Le Pont du Nord*, one of these texts is *Don Quixote*: even if Rivette hadn't spelled this out in a director's statement, it wouldn't be hard to see something of Quixote in Baptiste, from our first glimpse of her riding into town on her motorcycle like a knight on horseback. Like Quixote, Baptiste is a high-principled adventurer of no fixed abode—and Quixote's notion that the world is under the thrall of an evil enchanter is paralleled in her theory of the "Maxes," thuggish servants of the system who lurk around every corner. Ultimately, she even has a dragon to slay in the form of a playground slide that belches fire, a vision shared with the viewer via the film's sole "special effect."

Yet Baptiste isn't *just* Quixote, any more than Marie is simply the loyal yet sceptical Sancho Panza. Contrary to what we might have expected, it's Marie who expounds the rules of the Game of the Goose, interpreting a map of Paris pilfered from Julien; Baptiste sits by listening intently, every inch the faithful pupil, each of them munching on an apple in turn. Truth and illusion by this point appear interchangeable, which isn't so far from what happens in live-action movies generally: the camera records actuality while transmuting it into something else. Such is one way to understand what is meant by "the magic of cinema."

In the director's statement mentioned above, Rivette observes that every film is an "adventure film"—meaning firstly the adventure of filmmaking itself, where the outcome is never wholly foreseeable, however carefully things are planned.[4] Any creative pursuit might qualify as such an adventure, but a recording device adds an extra dimension (as children tend to grasp instinctively, treating the act of recording as a game in its own right). Reproduced on screen, the most ordinary settings become archetypal, pregnant with generalised meaning: the Bridge, the Labyrinth, the Inn. Likewise, the moment we step in front of a movie camera, our actions cease to be purely ours: they belong equally to a counterpart we may later view with bafflement and even outrage, as if a mirror reflection had taken on a life of its own. A doppelgänger, an Other.

4 Jacques Rivette, "Director's Statement," trans. Craig Keller. In *Le Pont du Nord* DVD booklet, 13.

5

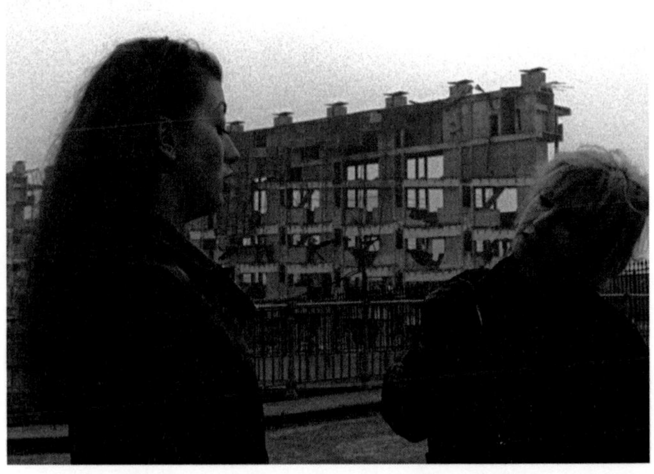

Le Pont du Nord is a tale of autumn, with Marie's red-blonde hair the colour of leaves about to fall, her red scarf adding a further flare of colour against grey buildings and grey skies. We seem to be entering the story at the wrong moment, after the real action is over and done with, whatever there was of it. What remains is a half-abandoned city where the freedom on offer is mainly of a negative kind—the freedom to search for spaces to use as hideouts, or for salvageable fragments amid the rubbish. Thus, the lightness of the film is founded on melancholy: if nothing has much consequence, it's because the game is already lost, even supposing the prize was more than a mirage to begin with.

No turning back the clock, after all. "The Grave isn't so sad, since you go back to the beginning," Marie tells Baptiste, recounting the original rules of the Game of the Goose as they pore over their board or map. But these rules are centuries old, and things have changed. "Nowadays, if you fell in the Grave, that would be the end." Baptiste has no comeback for this—and however whimsical the terms of the discussion, there's enough of a chill in the air to suggest the film's game is indeed being played for keeps (unlike in the suspended idyll of *Céline et Julie*, where the heroines end more or less as they began).

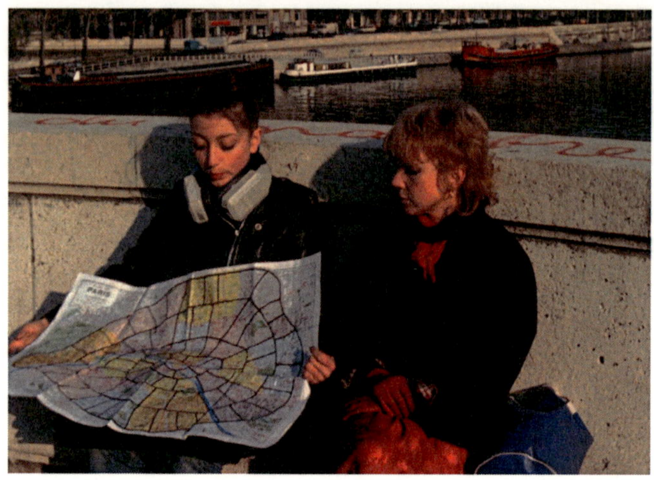

This brings home that play in itself is not a frivolous matter (something Rivette may have learned from his master Howard Hawks). On the contrary, the spirit of play is what enables survival, at least in the short term. Marie has some of the gallantry of a Marlene Dietrich heroine—stylish in spite of all, her jauntiness masking a knowledge that her time will soon run out. As a representative of youth, Baptiste puts up a parallel resistance to the reality principle, balancing on the edge of a canal, or skipping between railway sleepers with the wilfully narrowed focus of a child past her bedtime. Likewise, the stars who play these characters seem caught up in their rapport in the moment, independent of any third party—whether Rivette himself, or the eventual audience for the film, we who monitor their every move from the future, like so many Maxes.

6

Still more than in other Rivette films, everything in *Le Pont du Nord* seems in flux. This is true not just of the story and the characters, but of Paris itself, represented as a city under construction, like the London of *The Long Good Friday* (John Mackenzie, 1980), where the landmarks might turn out to have vanished if the protagonists retraced their steps. The final showdown occurs on a bridge over a canal, a public arena like the main street in a Western, pitting Baptiste against the original Max (Jean-François Stévenin), who may be the Mabuse pulling the strings or just another henchman. She slips into her kung fu stance; he takes a moment to drape his coat over a railing, then shows unexpected agility in fending her off, calling out cheerful advice as he does so ("It's a fight, but it's life too, you have to breathe"). Are they on the same side after all, meaning everything we've witnessed was just a charade? If so, does this mark the final collapse of the fiction, or a doubling down? Abruptly, the image is overlaid by a grid resembling the sights of a rifle, hinting at the possible intervention of some unseen and unnamed force monitoring the action from afar. As the one-time foes bow to each other, the camera pans away to a half-demolished building on the bank, a grey chaos resembling a modernist sculpture or a stack of puzzle pieces waiting to be put together. Time to start again . . .

Conall Cash

No Messing with Love: *À nos amours* (1983)

By the beginning, it's all over. When we meet Suzanne (played by Sandrine Bonnaire in her first film role), the time of love and happiness that she briefly shared with her boyfriend Luc—a love without jealousy, a love seemingly unblemished by the physical awkwardness and insistence of desire—is already past. This ideal past cannot be filmed: our first sight of Suzanne and Luc together, near the start of the film, is already marred by a distance that neither we nor they really understand, a distance somehow related to an emerging sexual desire. Suzanne's subsequent relationships and encounters will only echo this love that was damaged beyond repair before we came in. Of Suzanne and Luc's happy time, what do we learn? One hour and eighteen minutes in, at her last meeting with Luc, when she is about to marry someone else, Suzanne tells him: "The only time I was happy, it was in . . . in Courchevel, you remember? I was so happy I felt like I was dreaming. And that's why I wanted to die with you, on the toboggan."

Between happiness and death, Maurice Pialat's *À nos amours* will pursue the violence and the passion of a life lived in relation to—in search of, or in the desire to forget—these heightened, unfilmable states of surrender and abandon that can never quite be occupied, can never quite be ours. Another Maurice, the philosopher Merleau-Ponty, described the experience of an embodied life without self-conscious reflection as "a past that has never been present."[1] Such is Pialat's happiness, one whose

1 Maurice Merleau-Ponty, *Phenomenology of Perception*, trans. Donald Landes (Routledge, 2012), 252.

absence and whose echo haunt every frame, like a life haunted by a death that will return us to this unreflective state.

If an inarticulable happiness and an uninhabitable death are the forces pushing this cinema to its expression, it will have to create its own forms, or find them in the margins of the history of cinema and art. As Jean-Pierre Gorin has noted, Pialat positions his work in rejection of two prevailing images of French cinema: on the one hand, he refuses any connection to the *nouvelle vague*, due to what for him is its intellectualism, the winking cleverness which puts it at a distance from emotion and truth; but what he seeks also rejects the proper, self-serious "cinéma du papa" which was the object of ire for the New Wave filmmakers.[2] Pialat will find something of a model for his rough, bodily cinema in an earlier moment in French cinema, that of the 1930s, particularly in the early films of Jean Renoir. A cinema excited by the expressive powers of the body, a cinema attuned to this expressivity, ready to take what it finds, unsure of where it is going. "Je savais même pas ce que je faisais" ("I didn't even know what I was doing"), Suzanne will say recurrently throughout *À nos amours* when recounting significant moments in her life. Pialat's cinema wants to live in the space of this unknowing, to honour it, to dedicate itself to it (this film's title—perhaps uniquely in the history of cinema—is a dedication, addressed "to our loves"). Never to master it.

Countering the institution of French cinema, *À nos amours* also runs counter to three other great institutions: the school, the theatre, and the family. This is a film about education; about a young woman's sentimental education, and about the role of performance in this educational process: in learning how to perform, to act oneself out, to express one's being and one's character, does one get closer to or further from one's

2 Jean-Pierre Gorin, "Jean-Pierre Gorin on *À Nos Amours*", produced by Alexandre Mabilon, *The Criterion Channel*, accessed August 21, 2025.

own truth? The film begins with a rehearsal, as Suzanne repeats her lines (in French, a rehearsal is a *répétition*, signalling that one must repeat one's performance before one is ready to stage it, that the first time is never really the first time) for a performance of Alfred de Musset's 1834 play *On ne badine pas avec l'amour*, known in English as *No Trifling with Love.*[3] Suzanne is playing Camille, whose beloved Perdican has committed the grave wrong of "trifling with love," falsely declaring his affections for the innocent Rosette, who dies of heartbreak when she learns that he only has eyes for Camille. Camille places moral virtue above her own desire, leaving her beloved with these blunt final lines: "She is dead. Goodbye, Perdican." Suzanne will rehearse these lines with Michel, a friend of her older brother, who will tell her to inject them with more passion. In a final ironic blow to the moralism of Musset's play, *À nos amours* will end with Suzanne leaving her husband for this same Michel ("the one with the big nose" is the way Suzanne's father distinguishes him from the other men in her life) on a plane to San Diego.

If Musset's play wishes to use the theatre to educate through moral lessons, in *À nos amours*, no punishment and no judgement are meted out to those who "trifle with love." Here, the chaos of life and the callousness with which people treat each other, for reasons they scarcely understand, are brought to no moral or narrative resolution, and Pialat's film is an assault upon the rules of art represented by Musset's play, upon the idea that certain meanings, actions, and conclusions are appropriate to art while others are not. Through this, it is an assault upon the idea that an appropriately ruled art can teach the rules of life, of which Musset stands as a canonical figure—Musset, the supremely orderly, supremely French writer,

3 Alfred de Musset, *No Trifling With Love*, trans. Raoul Pellissier, in *The Complete Writings of Alfred de Musset* (Edwin C. Hill Company, 1905), Volume 3, 207–73.

of whose work Arthur Rimbaud wrote, "It is all French, namely detestable to the highest degree."[4] An educational theatre, a national theatre, a theatre of lessons, countered by a cinema of bodies and energies which reason and morality can barely keep up with, let alone educate or master.

And yet, in its own way, the film takes Musset's title quite seriously. Love, here, is not something one can ignore—in Pialat's version, it might better be translated as "No Messing with Love." Destroy yourself and others, destroy your relationships and your family and your own life all you like: you won't be able to get away from the wound that love has inflicted upon you, since before you were ever conscious of it. This attention to the primal wound of a love we cannot recapture is central to Pialat's treatment, his countering, of that other institution at the heart of *À nos amours*: the family.

Nicole Brenez writes that *À nos amours* is a film "about the mutual difficulty of parents and their children in admitting that the Other can have a body."[5] But what is it about the other generation's body that is so threatening? In an early scene, Suzanne is talking with a boy she's just had sex with (as always, we come in after the fact, missing the moment of intensity, and linger in the aftermath, with this boy who remains unnamed and whom we won't see again). When he speaks matter-of-factly about his mother's looks and aging body, Suzanne remarks that she could never speak about or look at her parents that way. What appears so threatening, confusing, and revolting in this boy's frank words about his mother is the *desacralisation* of the other's body—of the parent's body for the child, and the child's body for the parent.

4 Arthur Rimbaud, "Letter to Paul Demeny, 15 May 1871," in *Complete Works, Selected Letters: A Bilingual Edition*, trans. Wallace Fowlie (University of Chicago Press, 2005), 379.

5 Nicole Brenez, *On the Figure in General and the Body in Particular: Figurative Invention in Cinema*, trans. Ted Fendt (Anthem Press, 2023), 96.

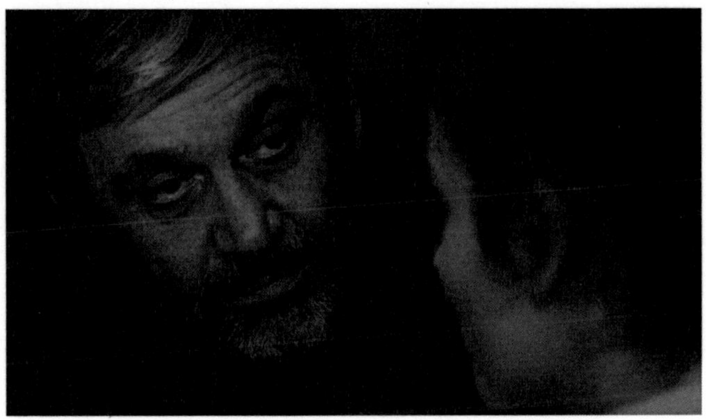

Within the family space, embodied relations are sacred, archetypal, defined by a lack of distance and a lack of need for personal autonomy or the expression of a separate desire. This sacrality is what becomes suffocating, both to Suzanne and to her father, who leaves the family abruptly a third of the way through the film. As Pascal Bonitzer writes, evoking a famous Deleuzian phrase: father and daughter are united in their shared capacity to "trace a line of flight," to pursue their own unnameable desire through a continual departure, rather than responding to the crisis of the sacred family home by broiling in resentment, in the excruciating and intoxicating suffering of blame and accusation, as do Suzanne's brother and mother.[6] By being in touch with not knowing, with a desire that will only take them further from home and from domestication by others, Suzanne and "le père," as she calls him, find their own strange way back to the sacred, to a place of giving and acceptance and letting go of their own power and mastery. We see this in the film's two scenes of father and daughter together, where an intimacy becomes possible

6 Pascal Bonitzer, "C'est vous qui êtes tristes." *Cahiers du cinéma* no. 354 (December 1983), 7. My translation.

precisely at the moment of departure—first his, and then, at the end of the film, hers, on that plane to San Diego.

To what end does *À nos amours*' counter-institutional movement, its splintering of so many norms of artistic and social institutions, tend? Radicals dream of abolishing institutions, of replacing their alienating, ossified forms with new, true expressions of our humanity—for to be radical, as Marx reminds us, is to go to the root, and for human beings, the root is humanity itself.[7] By uprooting the institutions we've inherited, this dream goes, we can create rational institutions that align with our true needs and desires, as the rational beings we are. The theatre, the school, the family: all of these institutions involve a sacred, mythic authority structure that the radical wishes to tear down and abolish (political antitheatricality runs from Plato's *Republic* to the Puritans of the English Civil War), replacing their representational function (the actors on stage representing reality to the audience; the teacher or the father representing the power and authority of the state) with organs of direct, communal self-expression.[8] Such a world will have no need of the sacred, for it will have mastered its energies through collective self-knowledge. In going to the root of humanity, radical critiques of institutionality sketch out their hopeful images of a new humanity, a humanity finally at one with itself.

But Maurice Pialat is no radical, and he doesn't film dreams. The happiness of pure life is an unfilmable dream on the edge of death, and no good, rational institution will grow from its roots. The critique of the theatre, the critique of educational institutions, the critique of the family—all will have

7 Karl Marx, "A Contribution to the Critique of Hegel's Philosophy of Right," in *The Marx-Engels Reader*, ed. Robert C. Tucker, (Norton, 1978), pp. 53–65.

8 Jonas Barish, *The Antitheatrical Prejudice* (University of California Press, 1981), and Justin Clemens, "'Yet Once More': John Milton's *Lycidas* as an Assault on the Ordinary," *Philosophies* no. 9 (2024), 131.

to remain difficult, in a condition of difficulty (for Bonitzer, Pialat's lesson is that life, like art, is "an obscure and difficult struggle").[9] The most radical dream of all—that of abolishing the family—is a dream of full desacralisation. In this dream, the mystery of embodied entanglement, of a debt to others that reaches beyond what we know and what we can economise (for how can we ever define or knowingly articulate and add up what we owe to our parents, or to our children?) is tamed by reason, by a rational economy of relations without remainder, without unmasterable debts or irretrievable losses. Call it a world of universal love, or a world where parents and their children address each other as "citizen"; call it heaven or call it hell—either way, what it is is a world without difficulty, without the struggle and the beauty that propel us towards art. One might call it, as it would surely like to call itself, a world without sadness, and Suzanne's father's thunderous declaration, via Van Gogh, is the film's final answer to this: "La tristesse durera toujours"—"Sadness will last forever." The saddest of all are those who dream of an end to sadness.

The principle of difficulty running through Pialat's work is most vividly on display in the scene in which he, in the role of the father, utters this statement upon making his unexpected return to the family home. Arriving in the midst of a dinner party—what seems to be a marriage celebration for Suzanne—among family and friends, who are all now in various states of inebriation, the father arrives to show a prospective tenant around the apartment, before sitting down, uninvited and clearly unwelcome, to try some of the food, glorying in the discomfort he is creating. The complacency of the group, in their intellectual debates and sexual innuendo, is overturned by the father's contemptuous gaze upon them, in a performance clearly relished by the famously surly Pialat.

---

9 Bonitzer, "C'est vous qui êtes tristes," 7.

Legend has it that this sudden arrival was unknown to the cast in advance, such that the shocked and defensive reactions of the other characters are expressions of the actors' real bewilderment. The difficulty and chaos of a scene like this one is achieved not through sheer improvisation, but through the interjection of an unpredictable element into what might otherwise work as a more or less conventional, narratively functional scene. Sometimes this element is subtle and minor, as in Suzanne and her father's earlier conversation about her lost childhood dimple—what the film's director of photography, Jacques Loiseleux, calls "this little extra thing, this little malfunction happening somewhere, this little incident," which Pialat and his team are always chasing.[10] But here, at the most explosive point in the film, it is embodied in the unnerving and frankly dangerous physical presence of the father, of Pialat-as-father.

If this savage climax offers a kind of return and revenge of the paternal law, it does not lead to any safely conservative conclusion or resolution. Pialat-as-father is less the figure of bourgeois paternal authority of a conventional psychoanalysis than he is the vengeful father of Freud's *Totem and Taboo*, returning from the dead to remind the living of their unpaid, forever unpayable debts.[11] This paternal law never 'wins,' never settles the social world into a pacified order—rather, its incessant, undying demand punctures a hole in the fabric of this world, leaving it in pieces. The disordered, elliptical narrative of *À nos amours*—a film in which what might have been crucial events happen off-screen and are alluded to only in passing, like the toboggan ride at Courchevel—becomes the form appropriate to this world that is at once haunted by lack and driven by an intense vibrancy (what Jacques Fieschi calls Pialat's "contradictory dialogue between the nihilism of

10 Interviewed in *L'Œil humain* (*The Human Eye*, Xavier Giannoli, 1999).

11 Sigmund Freud, *Totem and Taboo*, trans. James Strachey (Routledge, 1950).

his vision and the physical health of his cinema"), both of which express Pialat's refusal of the reign of knowledge, and the institutional forms that establish themselves around it.[12]

"Sadness will last forever" becomes another way of saying "No messing with love"—love's wound cannot be healed through knowledge, or through a proper succession of institutional power from one generation to the next, whether that succession be conservative or revolutionary. *À nos amours*, like any great work of art, is a film one spends one's lifetime learning to be able to see, to simply see what it shows us—not to look at it for the conventions it doesn't fulfil, not to treat its vitality and its irresolution as signs of generic 'grittiness'—and to follow Suzanne in her perpetual flight from the familial shackles of knowledge. Forever singular, forever difficult, Pialat's work is vital to everything that can be called counter-institutional in French cinema.

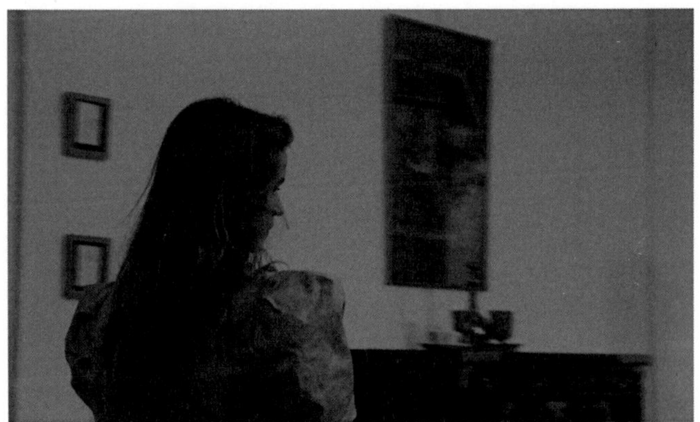

12 Interviewed in *L'Œil humain*.

Miranda Stanyon

Epigones and Enfants: *L'Amour fou* (1969)

L'Amour fou is sometimes regarded as Jacques Rivette's lost masterpiece. It has certainly been rarely screened to date, and remains understudied, largely because the four-hour version of the film was disowned by the production company, and a two-hour cut made at their behest was in turn disdained by the director. The original full-length film has existed only in one fragile copy, wheeled out at occasional film festivals and circulated on grainy bootlegs that help to give it a fetish value. A light air of conspiracy attaches to the film's scarcity—there's the select company that might appreciate it; the devoted *Sitzfleisch* needed to sit through it; even the hushed difficulty or occasional impossibility of discerning what is being said and done on a blurry screen. All this increased the pleasure of taking part in an amateur screening with a select company of viewers—only a few of whom didn't return after the interval—during the series of screenings and discussions Conall Cash hosted around the French New Wave and its aftermath.

Our use of an interval serendipitously conformed to Rivette's own views on filmgoing. "[F]or me," he once explained, "the most important point is when everyone goes to take a leak."[1] The interval Rivette structured into *L'Amour fou* partly reflected his "feeling that, physically, it was unbearable" to sit through the four-hour cut.

1 Jacques Rivette, "Time Overflowing," interview by Jacques Aumont, Jean-Louis Comolli, Jean Narboni and Sylvie Pierre, trans. Amy Gateff. In *Rivette: Texts and Interviews*, ed. Jonathan Rosenbaum (British Film Institute, 1977), 28. Originally published in *Cahiers du cinéma* no. 204 (September 1968).

> The interval is also the point where we pretend to be nice to the viewer and to give him back his freedom. So he does whatever he wants; if he wants to go away, he goes [...]. It should be like in the theatre, where you can leave in the middle—which I do, very often. On the other hand, I would like those who stay to stay right through to the end; I even think the doors ought to be locked. Going to see a film must be a contract—an act and a contract.[2]

Rivette did not specify what should happen to people who arrive late to a film. Nonetheless, belatedness is central to *L'Amour fou*, as we will see, and the film allows even eager beavers to feel they have missed something from the outset. The "After the New Wave" colloquium in March 2023, with its exploration of belatedness in French cinema, had alerted me to this theme more generally in post-New Wave cinema. Rivette is something of an icon in this regard—while a foundational figure of the New Wave, he would only become fully established as an auteur after that movement's peak had passed.

This made it fitting that our screening may have been one of the last occasions when the film could be billed as "lost" or "rarely screened": when we began discussing the event, there were rumours that a French production company was remastering *L'Amour fou* for a Blu-ray and DVD release, and on the evening that we met I learnt that the film had been digitised by another company and screened a week earlier at Cannes. Pipped at the post, we could nonetheless tell ourselves that we were at the vanguard of the revival in interest and scholarship that will surely follow this rerelease, given the revelatory sharpness and detail visible in the snippets that could already be seen online through

2 Ibid, 28–29.

the festival website. And if we were late, then we were in good company . . .

As someone who works primarily on the eighteenth century, I had been drawn to this riveting (pardon the pun) film by an interest in the Trojan woman Andromache, a figure who appears in works by Homer, Euripides, Seneca, Virgil, and others. *L'Amour fou* telescopes two moments in Andromache's long reception history that originally lay just over three hundred years apart: Jean Racine's neoclassical drama *Andromaque* (1667) and the shabby-chic world of post-1968 experimental theatre. If, as Jonathan Rosenbaum writes, "the entire body of Rivette's work can be read as a series of evolving reflections on the cinema," then the same could be said of Rivette's work in relation to the theatre.[3] *L'Amour fou* marks Rivette's first development of many future hallmarks of his work, especially duration and the use of open-ended, semi-scripted or improvised structures. It was, however, his third full length film (just as *Andromaque* was Racine's third play, and his first smash-hit), and his third rendering of a theatrical work. *Paris nous appartient* (*Paris Belongs to Us*, 1959) represented a staging of Shakespeare, and his banned film adaptation of Diderot's *La Religieuse* (*The Nun*, 1966) was developed after Rivette had directed a stage play based on the novel.

The film club screening thus offered a chance to think about Racine alongside a director who was himself a sharp interpreter of neoclassical myth and a powerful critic of theatre (as of film and indeed music), and to share initial thoughts about what is both the centre of *L'Amour fou* and something curiously displaced within it: the figure of Andromache herself.

3 Jonathan Rosenbaum, "Introduction" to *Rivette: Texts and Interviews*, ed. Jonathan Rosenbaum (BFI Books, 1977), 1.

Racine's *Andromaque*

The film centres on rehearsals for a production of *Andromaque*, directed by young thespian Sébastien (Jean-Pierre Kalfon), who also casts himself as the play's leading man opposite his wife Claire (Bulle Ogier). We watch their relationship and equilibrium unravel after Claire quits the play, ruffled by Sébastien's direction and by the presence of a film crew he has allowed to document the production process. The film is both a great remediation of the theatre by film and a running commentary on two modes of film, fiction and documentary, which are juxtaposed visually by the interplay between the 35mm footage used by Rivette's own (invisible) crew and 16mm footage used by real-life documentary filmmaker André S. Labarthe and his crew, often visible as they man their equipment or interview actors.

Racine's play needed no introduction for French audiences in the 1960s. Rivette chose it precisely as an old staple of the theatrical repertoire, one that simultaneously allows the viewer to orient herself via brief fragments of the play and that can show a troupe returning to a classic and trying to liberate it for experimentation. We see this experimentation principally in struggles over declamation: how to deliver Racine's grand Alexandrines—potentially monotonous six-stress lines in rhyming couplets, whose status in French roughly parallels Shakespearean blank verse. While the polish and high style of Racine's verse gave him a bad name, Rivette and his actors were soon absorbed by the "savagery" hidden beneath—and in—the Alexandrines' poise: "words that hurt, that torture," Rivette called them. "A true performance of Racine would be [...] nearly unbearable," he thought: "each line is full of incredible wickedness and savagery and clarity and daring. He really is a mad writer, one of the great sick authors of French literature."[4]

4 Ibid, 23.

Outside France, Racine's play does need some further introduction. Set in the aftermath of the Trojan War, it tells the story of Andromache, the widow of the Trojan hero Hector and mother of his son Astyanax. Regarded as the heir of Troy, Astyanax animates the action while never appearing on stage. He and his mother are captives and slaves of Pyrrhus, ruler of Epirus and the son of the dead Greek hero Achilles, Hector's killer. The play is structured by a classic *Liebeskette* of unrequited passions and rivalries. Loyal to Troy, Andromache (played in Sébastien's production by Célia) is loved by Pyrrhus (played by Sébastien), who is loved by his fiancée Hermione (played by Claire, and then by Sébastien's ex-girlfriend Marta), who is loved by Orestes (played by Yves). Racine begins with Orestes' arrival as an ambassador from the Greeks. They demand that Pyrrhus allow Astyanax's death, or risk provoking war with the other Greeks. Pyrrhus in turn presents Andromache with an ultimatum: marry him, or sign her son's death warrant. Secretly, Orestes hopes Pyrrhus *will* marry Andromache and leave Hermione to him. Hermione vacillates between passionate loyalty to Pyrrhus and plotting vengeance against him. The play ends with Pyrrhus's murder, Hermione's suicide, and Orestes' descent into madness. Only the implacable Andromache survives, crowned as queen of Epirus.

The bare plot of the play draws to the surface a number of parallels between life on and off stage in *L'Amour fou*: Sébastien is Pyrrhus the leader/lover, and sometimes also resembles Orestes, threatened with madness. Claire is the scorned, jealous, suicidal Hermione, and sometimes the detached, mournful widow Andromache, seeming to live in a world apart from the other players—"captive, always sad, a burden to [herself]," as Andromaque puts it in Racine's play. Indeed, Rivette claimed that he and Jean-Pierre Kalfon found the "analogies" between play and film scenario so plentiful, "facile," even "annoying," that during editing any "too obvious" parallels were broken up.[5] Yet Racine's play remains crucial to the film's themes and problems, prominent among them belatedness, generations, liberation, and displacement.

Belatedness, Repetition, and Regression

Belatedness is the condition of Racine's characters. Living in the aftermath of the Trojan war, all but Andromaque are children of the war's great warriors, leaders, and beauties, striving to live up to their legend. Belatedness is also the condition of our entry into *L'Amour fou*: the film starts with a moment of disarray, in need of an explanatory flashback—marked by the sound of Sébastien literally rewinding a tape. The flashback, which takes up the rest of the film, begins with the moment that Claire quits the production: a problem has just blown up, but we arrive too late to see it brewing. We are going over old ground but without a clear perspective emerging. Repetition and its interruption are guiding threads as we follow the increasingly warping daily habits of the married couple—but also as we watch the *répétitions* (rehearsals) of the play.

A psychological kin to repetition, regression was central to *Andromaque* for Rivette. He saw Racine's play as moving from men talking politics to women talking love, until "little by little, the adult characters disappear and the fifth act is really the act of the *enfants terribles* [Orestes, Hermione, and Pyrrhus], which can only lead to childish actions, to suicide and madness."[6]

5 Ibid, 11.

6 Ibid, 23.

Generations and family

Regression leads us to the theme of families, both literal and metaphorical. *L'Amour fou* is a film replete with infantile imagery, in which screaming babies, babushka dolls, puppy dogs for adoption, and meals apparently made largely of dairy products (even granting the well-known French penchant for yogurt) all surface like symptoms. Literal older and younger generations are largely absent from the action proper: Claire and Sébastien live almost entirely among coeval *enfants*, and they are radically ambivalent about the parental roles they might be called on to play. Claire neglects the kitten her husband brings home and pretends it has died; she makes a half-hearted attempt to steal a puppy belonging to a sad-eyed breed which, according to Sébastien, looks like her, while Sébastien refuses to be a "metteur-en-scène papa" ("daddy director"), rather unsuccessfully.

Influenced by then-contemporary psychoanalytic approaches to Racine, the treatment of age and family in the film is not—or not just—about archetypal plots and timeless psychological struggles.[7] It is tempting to see it as a mark of what one actress called Rivette's "*porosity* in relation to the epochs through which he passed": in this case, a rather troubled reflection on the tail end of the 1960s, with its explosive energy, experimentalism and rebellion in youth culture.[8] *L'Amour fou* is sometimes seen as celebrating the spirit of '68, keeping alive the revolution. But the intertext of Racine's *Andromaque*,

7 See Charles Mauron's *L'inconscient dans l'œuvre et la vie de Racine* (Ophrys, 1957) and Roland Barthes' *Sur Racine* (Éditions du Seuil, 1963); for a reflection on the trend see Leo Bersani's *A Future for Astyanax: Character and Desire in Literature* (Little, Brown and Co., 1969), 17–50.

8 Jeanne Balibar "Rivette Rock," interview by Joachim Lepastier, *Cahiers du cinéma* no. 720 (March 2016), 20. Quoted in Adrian Martin, "Jacques Rivette: The Great Manipulator," *Cinéaste* 41, no. 4 (2016): 5 (Martin's translation and emphasis).

with its gloomy treatment of a new generation, and the film's parental/infantile symbolism, can suggest a more dispiriting view of revolt.

Breaking Free

Liberation is firstly an aesthetic concern in the film. *L'Amour fou* was Rivette's first foray into processes and ideas of freedom that would continue to fascinate him: the ideal of a freely-evolving and unforced cinema; the interplay between chance and spontaneity on the one hand, and design or plot on the other (including plotting and conspiracy). Once called "the great manipulator," Rivette himself walked a vanishingly fine line between granting his actors wide freedoms and covertly controlling his films.[9]

Conveniently, Racine's play is dominated by the motifs of slavery, dependence, and freedom. The irony is meant to be that the unrequited passions of Orestes, Hermione, and Pyrrhus condemn them to a bondage far worse than that of Andromaque, the literal slave and remnant of a conquered nation. So there is a subtextual message about controlling the passions in order to be free, which sits oddly with Rivette's bohemian characters. Politically speaking, Racine's play can be seen as caught up with the goal of establishing strong, centralised, absolutist rule in the France of Louis XIV. The fiction here, as in a number of neoclassical plays, is that strong rule will guarantee liberties rather than enslaving its subjects.[10] It intersects with the older legal fiction that there are no slaves in France: that anyone stepping onto French soil is free, or

9 Bulle Ogier, interviewed in *Remembering Duelle*, special feature on *The Jacques Rivette Collection* (Arrow Academy, 2015). Quoted in Martin, "Jacques Rivette: The Great Manipulator," 9.

10 Cf. Ziad Elmarsafy, *Freedom, Slavery, and Absolutism: Corneille, Pascal, Racine* (Bucknell, 2003).

can claim freedom, even a Black slave from a French colony.[11]

What of the film's Andromaque? How is this slave portrayed? Here we enter territory somewhat less well charted in criticism on the New Wave and its aftermath.

"Absences and Displacements"

Racine's Andromaque is famously sidelined in the drama that bears her name: in its last act, she disappears entirely from the stage.[12] A similar fate befalls Rivette's Andromaque/Célia, who emerges on-stage in rehearsals only around half an hour into the film, and remains essentially a minor figure.

How can the film play off analogies between on- and off-stage relationships, and yet still marginalise the actor representing Andromaque? As I've suggested already, this is because Claire, after quitting the role of Hermione, acts not only as the scorned rival of the "new" Hermione—and so a repeated, concentrated figure of the rival—but also as a replacement Andromaque: Andromaque/Claire is the figure to whom Pyrrhus/Sébastien repeatedly professes his love, and who sits outside the normal sphere of action in the theatre. Like Andromaque, Claire is the character who refuses to play with the others, and who plots ways to leave Pyrrhus/Sébastien, and to be released from their oppressive relationship. Both seem to skirt death, and both escape it. In this way, the "real" Andromaque is displaced anew by the film's attention to Claire.

11 For a genealogy of this legal principle, see Sue Peabody, "An Alternative Genealogy of the Origins of French Free Soil: Medieval Toulouse," *Slavery & Abolition* 32, no. 3 (2011): 341–62.

12 This is true of Racine's revised edition of the play; the first edition saw her enter briefly to lecture Orestes and Hermione. Cf. Nicholas Hammond and Joseph Harris (eds.), *Racine's* Andromaque: *Absences and Displacements* (Brill Rodopi, 2019).

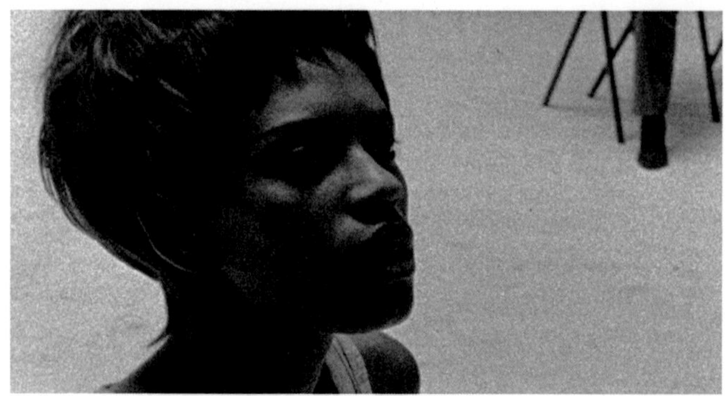

Figure 1: Célia rehearsing in the role of Andromaque

This real Andromache is "Célia"—the only name given to this actor, both by Sébastian and his cast, and in the film's credits (Figure 1). She is one of two Black women in the cast, the other being Andromaque's Trojan confidante, Céphise, played in Sébastien's production by "Madly" (Maddly Bamy, Figure 2). The striking colour-conscious casting by Rivette shapes other aspects of characterisation: a moment of casual "jokey" racism by Sébastien; the women's backstories as respectively a singer and dancer—sexy entertainers—while the others are presented as more serious actors, and so on. While several of Rivette's real-life cast members were associated with Marc'o's experimental theatre troupe, Maddly Bamy was indeed a dancer before she began acting. Having moved to Paris from Guadeloupe in the Antilles as a child, Bamy's other early film credits included "the dancing mulatto" (*La Piscine*, Jacques Deray, 1969) and "an Antiguan girl" (*L'Aventure c'est L'aventure*, Claude Lelouch, 1972). In the latter role she met Jacques Brel; she became his last partner, eventually writing several books about him. Ironically—though in striking repetition of the displacement of Racine's titular heroine—I have thus far been able to learn much less about Célia.

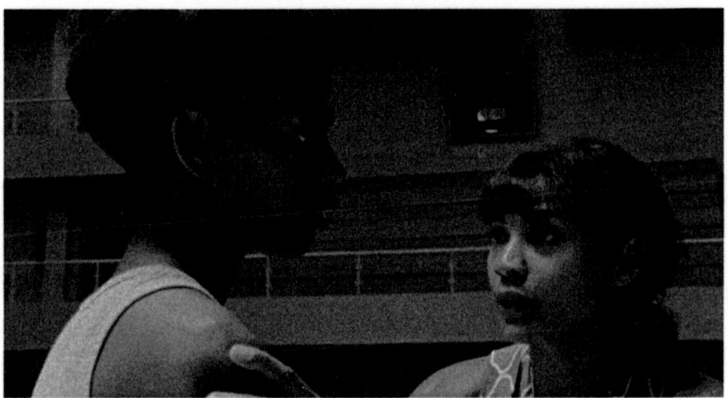

Figure 2: Célia (Andromaque) and Madly (Céphise) in rehearsal

While the logic of Sébastien's casting is never mentioned within the film, it might be seen to resonate with Rivette's oblique treatment of "exotic" territories and peoples historically colonised, enslaved, or exploited by France. And not just historically, of course: Algeria had gained independence just seven years earlier, after the war of 1954–62, and Guadeloupe is still a French department to this day. The island was taken as a possession of France in the seventeenth century, with the first slaves arriving from Africa in 1650, seventeen years before the premiere of *Andromaque*. How this history might surface in *L'Amour fou*, and what its traces might mean, are subjects open to further discussion, research, and review—especially in light of the newly restored digital version of the film. One might think more closely not only about the scenes in which Célia and Madly do (and don't) appear, and about Sébastien and Claire's private comments about the women, but also, for instance, about the décor of Sébastien and Claire's flat, with its tropical palm-tree fabric and Islamic-inspired geometric pictures—the site of the couple's climactic bout of absurdist play-acting and explosive destruction (Figure 3). Or Sébastien's private passion for the Afro-Cuban bongo-drums and other percussion, a soundworld which mirrors his choice of "exotic," untuned percussion in dress rehearsals for Racine's play.

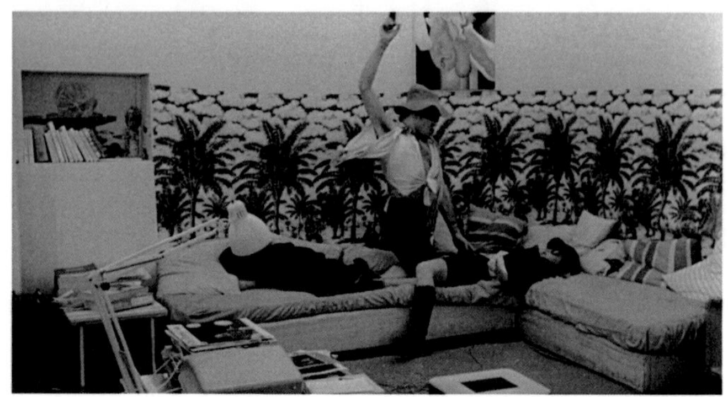

Figure 3: Director Sébastien and his wife Claire go wild at home

However one reads such scenes, it seems clear that *L'Amour fou* bears a distinctive witness to the still under-acknowledged presence of Black actors and artists in the orbit of the New Wave, and that the film makes an oblique intervention in French racial and (post)colonial politics. The New Wave has been accused of filming Paris "as if it is as white as a newly built home," and "gloss[ing] over the fact that not everyone living in Paris is white."[13] If so, Rivette's film is an exception to the rule, although a belated one, and certainly not one which emerges from nowhere. For one thing, beyond the now-canonical New Wave directors, Black and white filmmakers were already changing the representational space of France.[14] In the institution of the theatre, too, Rivette's casting choice

13 Wes Felton, "Caught in the Undertow: African Francophone Cinema in the French New Wave," *Senses of Cinema* no. 57 (December 2010).

14 Prominent examples are Paulin Soumanou Vieyra's *Afrique sur Seine* (1955), Ousmane Sembène's *La Noire de . . .* (1966) and Med Hondo's *Soleil Ô* (1967), alongside Edgar Morin and Jean Rouch's documentary *Chronique d'un été* (*Chronicle of a Summer*, 1961), which involved both Rivette and his collaborator

suggests parallels with contemporary Francophone postcolonial rewritings and restagings of the classics, as well as with the shaky beginnings of Black actors' recognition in the theatrical establishment.[15] Is Célia the first recorded Black actor to play Racine's Andromaque in France? Or the first to have been filmed in the role? Clearly, there is more to say and more to learn. But as a preliminary conclusion, we might say that, if Andromaque is marginalised or displaced in *L'Amour fou* in many ways, then this marginalisation—suggested by Racine and accentuated by Rivette—is not an accidental but a significant element in the film, crucial to its troubling interrogation of freedom and dependence.

---

and wife Marilù Parolini. Cf. e.g. Felton, "Caught in the Undertow." On "oblique" and "displaced" representations of French colonialism in other New Wave films, see Elizabeth Ezra, "Cléo's Masks: Regimes of Objectification in the French New Wave," *Yale French Studies* no. 118/119 (2010): 177–90, especially pages 185 and 187, and further scholarship referred to there. Recent scholarship on French colonialism and film more broadly, often indebted to the work of historian Benjamin Stora, includes Ahmed Bedjaoui, *Cinema and the Algerian War of Independence* (Palgrave, 2020); Jon Cowans, *Film and Colonialism in the Sixties: The Anti-Colonialist Turn in the US, Britain, and France* (Routledge, 2019); Delphine Robic-Diaz and Alain Ruscio, "Postcolonial Cinema, Song, and Literature: Continuity or Change? (1961–2006)," in Pascal Blanchard et al. (eds.), *Colonial Culture in France since the Revolution* (Indiana, 2014), 546–51.

15 Georges Aminel had joined the Comédie Francaise in 1967 as its first Black *pensionnaire*, and in 1968 played the role of Pyrrhus in *Andromaque* (first performance 21 April 1968); he would quit in dissatisfaction in 1972, just before being made a *sociétaire*.

Corey P. Cribb

An Ode to Headlessness: *Acéphale* (1968)

In many ways, Patrick Deval's debut feature film *Acéphale* is inextricably wedded to the historical moment of its production, exhibition, and reception. At 24 years of age, Deval had been intimately involved in the legendary radical student demonstrations that swept across Paris in the spring of 1968. Along with Laurent Condominas, and Deval's better-known counterpart Philippe Garrel, Deval had helped produce *Actua 1* (1968), a six-minute *actualité* documenting the violence which the young protestors suffered at the hands of the police. Mythologised as a genuinely collective work of radical film practice, *Actua 1* was long thought to be lost, before Garrel happened upon the negatives just over a decade ago; it would subsequently screen at the Cannes and Toronto film festivals in 2015. It was most probably during the events of May '68 that Deval was introduced to Sylvina Boissonnas, a militant leftist who dished out wads of cash from her family inheritance to produce a handful of low-budget avant-garde films. These films would come to be known collectively as the works of *Le groupe Zanzibar*, or simply Zanzibar. Having up to this point produced two shorts—*Zoé bonne* (1966) and *Héraclite l'obscur* (1967)—Boissonnas's patronage gave Deval the means and the creative freedom required to produce the 56-minute anomaly that is *Acéphale* without industrial backing.

As it happens, Deval himself claims to have had no knowledge that, alongside his own film, Boissonnas had funded works by many of his peers, remarking in a 2008 interview with *Senses of Cinema*:

> I never knew I was part of a group named Zanzibar when we were playfully producing *Acéphale*. Actually, it was only in the '80s, when coming back to France, that I learned my pals of the time—mainly Philippe Garrel, Daniel Pommereulle, Jackie Raynal, [and] Serge Bard—had done a movie with a cheque from this lady, Sylvina Boissonnas, and that the productions of this group in the year '68/'69 came to be called Zanzibar.[1]

Deval's ignorance of his own participation in what would be consecrated as a "collective" may be explained by his personal itinerary: after filming *Acéphale* in the summer of '68, he left France to travel across the United States, Mexico, and Morocco, before settling down in Indonesia and Japan. Unbeknownst to him, *Acéphale* premiered in 1969 at the Cannes Film Festival's inaugural *Quinzaine des réalisateurs* (Director's Fortnight)—itself a product of demonstrations at the 1968 edition of the festival led by Jean-Luc Godard and François Truffaut, for which the Zanzibar moniker was invented. The title is an ode to the letters of Arthur Rimbaud, who, despite being exceptionally well-travelled, never did make it to Zanzibar, yet spoke of it often as a utopian *terra incognita*.[2]

Although Deval never understood himself to be part of a film movement or collective (as Zanzibar is sometimes presented), his work sits comfortably alongside the other Zanzibar films, thanks to their shared investment in the solemn yet utopian idea that cinema could function as a tabula rasa by radically breaking with the medium's stylistic, performative, and narrative conventions. For the most part, the Zanzibar films do not explicitly tackle political issues; however, for Sally Shafto—whose short critical biography remains

1 Patrick Deval, "Deval in '68: An Interview with Patrick Deval," interview by Fergus Daly and Maxmilian Le Cain, *Senses of Cinema*, no. 48 (2008).

2 See Jackie Raynal, "Jackie Raynal Talks about a Life in Movies," interview by Janique Vigier, *Art Forum*, February 16, 2021.

the sole academic text on Zanzibar—they each subscribe to a quasi-political logic, commensurate with the "spirit of '68," according to which cinematic style is itself to be understood as a "visual ideology."[3]

Stylistically, *Acéphale* is notable for its accomplished cinematography (comprised of meticulous shot compositions and skilful, high-contrast lighting), affectless performances, opaque dialogue, and experimental sound design. Michel Fournier (who worked on many of Garrel's early films) was hired as the cinematographer, only to be replaced by Guy Gilles after Fournier quit the production in protest at an improvised scene in which an actor bites the head off a chicken, which does not feature in the final cut of the film.[4] The cast was made up of a selection of nonprofessional actors that Deval had assembled from his friends in the hippy or "dandy" community, including members of the London-based performance art group The Exploding Galaxy. The film was edited by Deval's then-girlfriend Jackie Raynal, whose own debut feature *Deux fois* (1968) screened alongside *Acéphale* in the Zanzibar showcase at Cannes.

Along with the surrealist literary review *Le Grand Jeu* (1928–30), *Acéphale*'s principal source of inspiration is George Bataille, Pierre Klossowski, and André Masson's journal of the same name, of which five issues were released between 1936 and 1939. Its title a French interpretation of the Greek word for "headless" (ἀκέφαλος), the journal is known for its sympathetic commentaries on Friedrich Nietzsche, its strong opposition to fascism (including the appropriation of Nietzsche's thought by the Nazis), and its valorisation of the idea of "the sacred" as a force linked to eroticism and death, drawing inspiration from the anthropologist Marcel

3 Sally Shafto, *The Zanzibar Films and the Dandies of May 1968* (Zanzibar USA, 2000), 12.

4 Patrick Deval, "Bel homme, adieu!" *Senses of Cinema*, no. 50 (2009).

Mauss. In an early sequence in the film, *Acéphale*'s nameless protagonist delivers a lengthy monologue in a lecture theatre populated by an audience of six seated attendees, made up of four adults and two children. Taken verbatim from Bataille's contribution to the inaugural issue of *Acéphale* the journal, this uncanny lecture becomes something of a manifesto that informs the film thereafter:

> It is time to abandon the world of the civilized and its light. It is too late to be reasonable and educated—which has led to a life without appeal. Secretly or not, it is necessary to become completely different, or to cease being. The world to which we have belonged offers nothing to love outside of each individual insufficiency [...] If it is compared to worlds gone by, it is hideous, and appears as the most failed of all. In past worlds, it was possible to lose oneself in ecstasy, which is impossible in our world of educated vulgarity [...] [M]en today profit [from civilization] in order to become the most degraded beings that have ever existed.[5]

As an alternative to the logic of this vulgar, individualistic world of civilised beings, Bataille identifies with Masson's drawing of a headless being with a maze embroiled on its stomach adorning the journal's cover, a dagger gripped by one hand and a flame radiating from the other. This being "who makes me laugh because he is headless," Bataille writes, and Deval's character reads, "is not me yet he is more myself than me [*plus moi que moi*]: his stomach is a labyrinth in which he has lost himself, loses me with him, and in which I discover myself as him, in other words as a monster."[6]

5 Georges Bataille, "The Sacred Conspiracy," in *Visions of Excess: Selected Writings 1927–1939*, trans. Allan Stoekl, with Carl R. Lovitt and Donald M. Leslie, Jr (Minnesota University Press, 1985), 179.

6 Ibid, 181 (translation modified).

Without attempting to reproduce this monstrous being, Deval's *Acéphale* seizes upon Bataille's radical call for a return to a state of reasonless, ecstatic monstrosity by a number of aesthetic means, with little by way of narrational guidance. Although it clearly has philosophical pretensions, *Acéphale* is, above all, a film made up of enigmatic imagery which evokes ritual, death, bohemian life, and what Deval describes as the "refusal of Western Civilisation" or "the end of white man."[7] The opening shot of the film depicts a man's head in extreme close-up. The camera tracks across the contours of his skull from one ear to another and then extends across his face, drifting in and out of focus as the whirring of an angle grinder occupies the soundtrack. We are then introduced to the young lecturer through a series of obscure close-ups filmed in a Parisian park. His head, captured by a tracking shot which begins side-on before circling around the back of his cranium, dances up and down in the frame like a galloping horse, accompanied by short, sharp, nondiegetic panting sounds and a discordant whirr that resembles the screams of an animal, but is more likely the sound of howling wind. Strangers glance at him as he passes, and we in turn regard his expressionless face, framed by his cascading hair, with no means of identification. These images of the head express something akin to the "nihilism of the face" that Gilles Deleuze identifies in Ingmar Bergman's *Persona* (1966), in which, the philosopher writes, "the principle of individuation ceases to hold sway."[8] Deval's head is a space not only free from reason but stripped of interiority, a passage which "opens me to a rapturous escape from the self."[9]

7 Patrick Deval, "Deval in '68."

8 Gilles Deleuze, *Cinema 1: The Movement-Image* (Bloomsbury, 2013), 111.

9 Bataille, "The Sacred Conspiracy," 181.

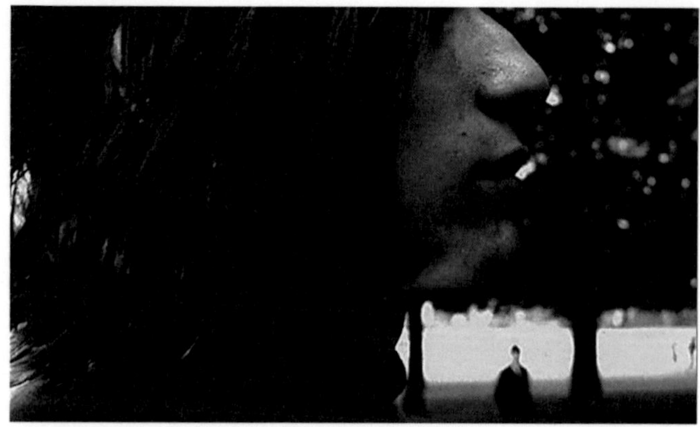

Acéphale is sometimes billed as a portrait of post-May '68 Paris, but a significant section of the film takes place in a rural area outside the city, where a band of hippies have seemingly taken refuge. Deval films this group warming themselves by a fire, their bodies nourished by what one character describes as "the absence of being." This is not, however, a film about convalescence in nature. Instead, it mobilises images and sounds of animal life to dissolve the border between the human being and its monstrous animal counterpart. In one memorable performance-art sequence, set to a chorus of flies, a man surfaces from a hole in the ground that has been covered over with dirt. As if born into an unfamiliar world, he looks around, makes a strange snaking motion with his hands, and then begins to crawl away, dragging himself across the dirt. We then see another actor wrapping himself in a thick, spider web-like substance. The buzzing of the flies is joined by a loop track featuring the caws of a bird, a man crying, and an off-key melody. To be headless, it would seem, is not merely to extinguish the light of reason, but also to recognise the discomforting animality of being which resides within us all.

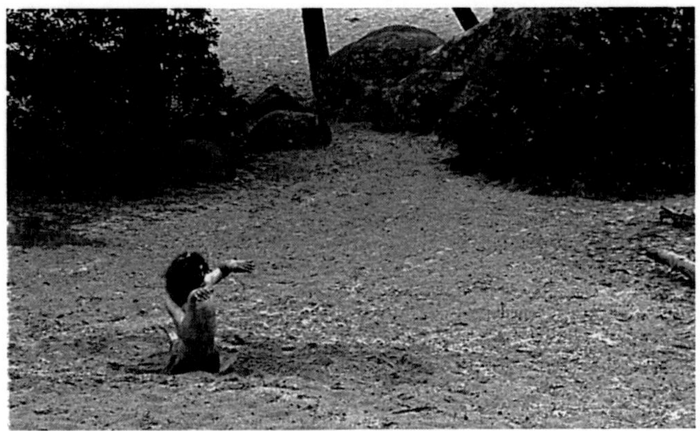

The remainder of the film is loosely structured around two locations: an abandoned train tunnel and a Parisian apartment. A remarkable, jerky tracking shot captures a group of youths as they run towards the light outside the tunnel, their momentum underscored by the whirrs of an unseen train. As they move into the daylight, each figure slows down and begins to stumble in an intoxicated manner before falling to the ground, where they lie lifelessly until the screen fades to white. As with Bataille, Deval seems fascinated by death as a kind of negativity that is unmasterable yet brimming with generative potential. In the following scene, the protagonist sneaks up on a woman walking alone at night, wraps his scarf around her neck, and begins to strangle her. Before she can yell out, he releases his grip and remarks, "Oh, sorry," walking away as if nothing had transpired. The scene is shocking, and offensive to today's sensibilities in the casualness with which it broaches gendered violence. At the same time, it is this staunch, transgressive quality—sometimes insensitive in its pursuit of any kind of "degradation" that the bourgeoisie might find offensive—that perhaps best represents the film's wager on freeing cinema from the shackles of both

Western epistemology and morality, much as, in the words of Bataille's text, "the condemned man escape[s] from his prison".[10] Indeed, Deval recalls that "the general mood in '68 drove us to plotting, underground, esotericism, and whatever could subvert, trouble, and erase the establishment," and this is what drew him to Bataille.[11] Above all, *Acéphale* is a film that, in its search for new modes of existence, embraces all those unwanted and violent parts of ourselves that we have neglected to recognise as human. It is a film that pursues the decapitation of reason by whatever means necessary.

10 Ibid, 181 (translation modified).
11 Patrick Deval, "Deval in '68."

Jack Keenan

Salvation and Civilisation: *L'Enfant sauvage* (1970)

François Truffaut's *L'Enfant sauvage* (*The Wild Child*) is based on the true history of Victor of Aveyron.[1] Victor was a so-called "feral child" who lived alone in a forest in south-central France from about age three to twelve. Just before the dawn of the nineteenth century, Victor was captured by a band of hunters who tracked him down in the woods of La Bassine in the region of Lacaune. He was placed in the custody of an old widow, from whom he quickly escaped. He then broke off for the mountains, "where he wandered about during the severity of a most vigorous winter, clad only in a tattered shirt."[2] By mid-January 1800, the cold proved too much for Victor. He sought shelter in the workshop of a dyer named Vidal. This marked his entry into the permanent custody of men—although he would escape their society a few more times, he would always return shortly after, either voluntarily or by force. From Vidal's workshop, he was sent to the orphanage of Saint-Affrique. From there, he was carted off to Rodez, where he was awaited by a professor of natural history named Bonaterre. Bonaterre conducted a five-month study, which resulted in the first scientific report published on the case.[3] Yet

1 For a comprehensive work on the historical case, see Harlan Lane's *The Wild Boy of Aveyron* (Harvard University Press, 1976).

2 Jean Marc Gaspard Itard, *An Historical Account of the Discovery and Education of a Savage Man* (Richard Phillips, 1802), 14.

3 For a reproduction of Bonaterre's report see pages 33–51 of Lane's *The Wild Boy of Aveyron.*

the time with Bonaterre was cut short when an edict from a government commissioner arrived, requesting Victor's immediate transport to the *Institution National des Sourds-Muets*, where he was to be studied by its director, the esteemed pioneer of sign language, Abbé Sicard.

However, it did not take long for Sicard and his colleagues—among them Philippe Pinel (portrayed in the film by Jean Dasté), the "father of modern psychiatry" and director at the Bicêtre hospital—to diagnose the boy with idiocy. Educating him was therefore impossible. Congenital idiocy presented an obstacle that education could not surmount. The prospect of his case shedding light on the "metaphysical problem" of determining the intelligence of a human being who grew up "entirely separated from individuals of his species" was dismissed.[4] He was not a true savage. He was an abandoned idiot forced by circumstance to become a savage. There was only one in this milieu who defended the idea that the reverse might hold: that Victor's idiocy was a result of his savagery, and that education could ameliorate the abandoned boy's condition.[5]

This was the opinion of a young physician who had been newly appointed at Sicard's institute. Dr. Jean Marc Itard thought that his colleagues had overestimated the boy's idiocy and underestimated the effects that the isolation from society had had on Victor's intelligence. He accepted that educating the boy would entail starting with the very basics, that he would have to—I quote from the film—teach Victor "*how to look and listen.*" With these convictions in his heart, Jean Itard took Victor into his home. For the next five years, the doctor

4 Itard, *An Historical Account*, 24–5.

5 Edward Seguin, *Idiocy: and Its Treatment by the Physiological Method* (William Wood & Co, 1866) 18–26.

and his housekeeper Mme Guérin would labour together in a noble attempt to care for and educate the *enfant sauvage*.

Itard speculated that Victor was abandoned at about age three. Nothing is known about Victor's parents, nor their reasons for abandoning him. Perhaps some hardship forced them to part with the boy, or perhaps it was his abnormal constitution—his congenital idiocy—that incited his abandonment. Whatever the cause, and whomever the parents, it seems that their intentions exceeded simple abandonment. The scar tissue of a long laceration across Victor's windpipe suggests that someone ran a knife through his jugular before leaving him for dead at the foot of the woods called La Bassine.

Miraculously, Victor survived. Dr. Itard conjectured that fallen leaves must have covered the wound, which together with muck blown by the wind created a seal around the laceration that stopped the bleeding and let it heal. It's as if Mother Nature took mercy on the wretched child and called upon her accidents to concoct a balm for his lacerated windpipe. One can imagine a convalescent Victor batting his eyelids open to that strange ceiling of soteriological leaves which would house him for the next eight years.

François Truffaut first came across the case in an edition of *Le Monde* in 1964. Immediately struck by the story, he dropped what he was working on at the time—a scenario for *L'Argent de poche* (*Small Change*, 1976), a film that would not see the light of day until the mid-seventies—and began to work with Jean Gruault (with whom he had already adapted *Jules et Jim*) on a screenplay which soon ballooned into a four-hundred-page manuscript. In the end, concerns about the film's length led Truffaut and Gruault to pare down their script to an austere 151 pages.[6]

6 Antoine de Baecque and Serge Toubiana, *Truffaut: A Biography*, trans. Catherine Temerson (Berkeley: University of California Press), 260–265.

The screenplay for *L'Enfant sauvage* was completed in 1968—a year of intense political fervour that culminated in a quasi-revolution which erupted in Paris in May of that year. Not incidentally, '68 was the year that Truffaut was at his most militant, spearheading the cause closest to his heart: the plight of maligned and abused children. In April of '68, he was asked to host a day-long radio programme devoted to himself, which he accepted on the condition that "the broadcast focus exclusively on the cause of abused children."[7] This passion of Truffaut's stems from his own experience as a neglected child.

Janine de Monferrand was just nineteen, and unmarried, when she gave birth to her first son. It was a scandalous pregnancy that sullied the reputation of Janine and her well-to-do Catholic family. Ashamed and unequipped for motherhood, she left the young François in the care of a wet nurse beyond the Parisian periphery. Hardly visited by his family, the *enfant* François spent his first three years in obscurity and neglect. Ostensibly abandoned, he became sick and emaciated. At the final hour, a chance visitation from his maternal grandmother saved the boy from the brink. Appalled at his paltry state and fearing for the worst, Geneviève de Monferrand adopted her estranged grandson and brought him into her home.

It should be stated that the influence of Geneviève de Monferrand upon her grandson was not merely as his saviour. She was also, among other things, his educator. She instilled in François his love of letters and higher culture. I'll quote from Antoine de Baecque and Serge Toubiana's biography of Truffaut to give a brief portrait of the woman:

> A former schoolteacher, [Geneviève] was a music lover and very well read. An occasional writer, she had penned a novel entitled *Apôtres* (*Apostles*) written in a very mannered style and permeated with mystical

7 Ibid, 262.

> fervour. Geneviève shared her passion for reading with François, taking him, at the age of five or six, on long walks through the Drouot neighbourhood, from bookstore to bookstore, and to the public library in the ninth arrondissement.[8]

The parallels between the lives of François Truffaut and Victor of Aveyron suggest that the former may have identified himself with the latter when he first read about Victor's case. Perhaps it was reading about that soteriological leaf—felled from the heavens by a chance gust of wind—which established Truffaut's identification with the boy.

Both abandoned at the tender age of three and saved by a roll of the dice, the parallel lives of Truffaut and the *enfant sauvage* are linked by a moment of salvation that arrived by chance. The chance visit that Geneviève de Monferrand paid to the young and emaciated François can be grafted, as it were, onto the balm that the forest concocted by luck—both resulted in the convalescence of a child who had been left to oblivion, and in his consequent adoption into a new home. There are thus grounds to speculate that Truffaut's great attachment to this case—the enthusiasm which seized him when he first read about it, and that in the end drove him to make this film—was the work of his (unconscious) primary process that forged an identification with Victor on the back of a metaphorical displacement that equated Truffaut's grandmother with the woods called La Bassine.

This equation—of grandmother with woods—must draw upon the myth of nature as a force of nurture in order to sustain its sense. The woods of La Bassine thus become both mother and home to Victor. There is an objective side to this idea: the woods did house Victor for eight years, and therefore in a certain sense "mothered" him. We might say that Victor was

8 Ibid, 5.

"raised by the woods" insofar as La Bassine's environmental conditions instructed him in developing the traits (his canine gait, acute sense of smell, imperviousness to climatic extremes, and so on . . .) that characterised his form of life therein. Yet it was not, for these reasons "nurturing mother nature" that raised Victor, but her wicked double: what Friedrich Nietzsche would call nature's "step-motherly mood." This "step-motherly" nature used her "cruel and merciless assaults" to force Victor into selecting the adaptive strategies that were most expedient to his survival within her *agon*[9]—a far cry from a sheltered upbringing within the *domus*.

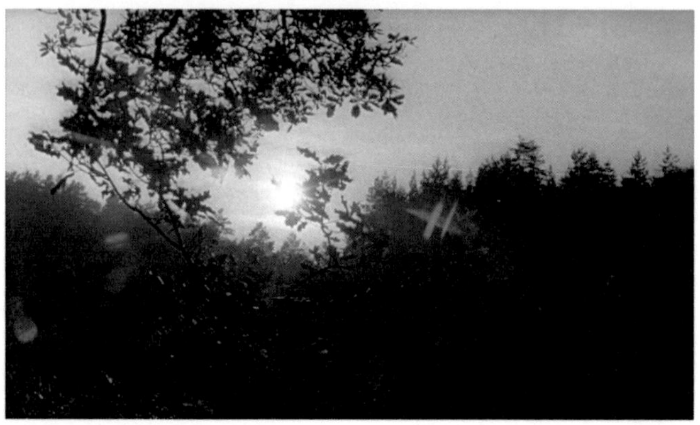

Truffaut himself was ready to admit as much in an essay he wrote on the genesis of his film: "Like Itard [...] I believe that the life [Victor] led [in the woods] was wretched, and the dozen scars on his body show perfectly well that he had to fight and maybe kill to survive."[10] Nonetheless, it is hard to recall

9 Friedrich Nietzsche, *Untimely Meditations*, trans. R.J. Hollingdale (Cambridge University Press, 2022), 130.

10 François Truffaut and Jean Gruault, "How I Made the Wild Child," in *The Wild Child*, trans. Linda Lewin and Christine Lémery (New York: Washington Square Press, 1973), 17.

a single moment in *L'Enfant sauvage* when the woodlands are given a bad look. There is hardly a grey sky among the film's dozens of bucolic vistas. From the get-go—before the opening credits have even ended—the audience is treated to only the most temperate impressions of nature. The serene warbling of summertime birds precedes the aperture-in to an opening sequence that flickers with dappled light and bucolic mildness. The woods of La Bassine are here imbued with the glimmering, deified quality in which one may (I think) glimpse the transferred trace of Truffaut's own good-natured grandmother.

But I do not want to make out that the film is so caught up in this idealisation that its treatment of nature is altogether uniform or univocal. Indeed, the contradiction between what the film "says"—at least in its more romantic moments—and what Truffaut says in his essay about the film is played out in the opening sequence's final shot. We see Victor perched up high in the fork of an oak tree. As the camera zooms out, he is enveloped by the tree's capillaries which seem to dissolve him in an embrace suggesting his nurture at nature's bosom. Yet if we look closer, we will see that Victor scratches himself while rocking incessantly back and forth: he is infected with parasites. What is yielded is an image that seems to state two contradictory propositions at once: *nature is benevolent* and *life is wretched.*

Evidently, *L'Enfant sauvage* was shot in the summertime, even though some of the historical events it depicts occurred during the winter. This transposition speaks to my larger argument: despite moments of nuance that crack with contradiction, the film is everywhere supported by cutaways to warm, benevolent nature. A pan to a window pouring vernal light; a zoom-out to reveal unforeseen canopies bearing pristine witness. The film is punctuated—thoroughly undergirded—by a reference to an idealised nature that betrays the transferred trace of Geneviève de Monferrand.

It is a curious fact that François received his famous last name from the man his mother married to rectify her reputation after the scandal of her son's birth out of wedlock (tragically, François' younger brother—fathered by this new husband—would only live for a few weeks).[11] Roland Truffaut had a good relationship with his stepson, despite the largely callous treatment his wife reserved for her unwanted child. François would move into the couple's cramped Parisian flat after Geneviève died when Truffaut was ten.[12] The combination of tight space, adolescent angst, and Oedipal tension made for a highly strung apartment. The years of teenage delinquency that resulted from this situation would later be made famous by their fictionalisation in Truffaut's feature-length debut *Les Quatre Cents Coups* (*The 400 Blows*, 1959).[13]

At this juncture, it is worthwhile to consider Truffaut's decision to play Dr. Itard in the film. It is easy enough to see in this decision a wish on Truffaut's part to replay or work through the teacher–student and father–son dynamics that run a thread through his œuvre. The film's dedication to Jean-Pierre Léaud (Truffaut's own *enfant sauvage*, the fourteen-year-old star of *Les Quatre Cents Coups*) certainly indicates that Truffaut was conscious of *L'Enfant sauvage*'s parallels with his life and work.

Truffaut insisted, against such interpretations, that the decision to play Itard was a purely pragmatic choice that allowed him to direct first-time child actor, Jean-Pierre Cargol, in the titular role as the "wild child" while in front of the camera. But this "pragmatic" explanation undermines itself insofar as it itself betrays Truffaut's wish to occupy the position of a benevolent father: he wishes to initiate Cargol into the world of cinema, just as Itard wishes to initiate Victor into the world of language.

11 Antoine de Baecque and Serge Toubiana, *Truffaut: A Biography*, 4.

12 Ibid, 10–11.

13 Ibid, 12–17.

Authority figures throughout Truffaut's life and work tend to approximate one or the other side of a dipole: abhorred masters on the one end, idealised saviours on the other. Roland Truffaut, André Bazin,[14] and Truffaut himself in relation to Jean-Pierre Léaud are all representatives of the saviour sequence, while Guy Decombe's hard-nosed schoolmaster in *Les Quatre Cents Coups* is the exemplar of the abhorred end of the spectrum. The position of Itard is ambiguous: he plays the saviour, yet must act the castrator. As Victor's educator, he attempts to put the boy through the wringer of "symbolic castration."

According to Lacanian psychoanalysis, speech presupposes symbolic castration, insofar as speaking demands the acknowledgement of a third term—"a virtual point of reference"[15]—which makes the relation that obtains between two speakers possible. This third term, Lacan's "Big Other," demands to be acknowledged as absolute—as the locus of the law which mediates and presides over the use of language. One is therefore always lacking when judged relative to this Big Other. Moreover, if—as is the case for someone learning to speak—the ordinary "little other" that one is talking to seems to know more than oneself, then they may take on a potent appearance which endows them with the Big Other's absolute and authoritative knowledge. This perception causes one's interlocutor to take on an overbearing appearance that painfully reminds a subject of their own impotence and lack of knowledge relative to the law. Castration is therefore unavoidable, for coming into a symbolic order always entails the acknowledgement of that order as authoritative,

14 On Truffaut's relationship with Andre Bazin, see Dudley Andrew's "Every Teacher Needs a Truant: Bazin and *L'Enfant sauvage*," in *A Companion to François Truffaut*, eds. Dudley Andrew and Anne Gilman (Wiley-Blackwell, 2013), 221–41.

15 Slavoj Žižek, *Virtue and Terror* (Verso, 2007), xxiv.

and the recognition of one's own lack relative to the locus of that authority.

The lack engendered by symbolic castration in turn becomes the impetus of desire. Desire is derivative of this lack, insofar as what propels desire is an object that promises to return what was lost in the process of castration. The castrated subject thus desires insofar as they wish to "refind" a lost object that never was. At bottom, desire is caused by a "hallucinated object" that is impossible to retrieve.[16] Castration therefore signifies a fate of eternal dissatisfaction. Being subject to desire means that one is forever propelled by wishes that are impossible to realise.

Is Victor a castrated subject? Or has he been merely 'domesticated'? He certainly seems to exhibit what you might call a "lack of lacking." When left to his own devices, he is not at pains to pursue his desires, and instead is happy simply dwelling in the canopy of a tree that he has climbed. He is not propelled on anguished quests after lost objects. He is content being carted around in a wheelbarrow across a gnarly paddock. Some readings of Lacan advance the idea that a "lack of lacking" is what distinguishes the position of an animal from that of a human subject.[17] Framed in these terms, Victor's subject position resembles that of a domesticated animal. However, it is unclear to what extent Victor "lacks lacking." It seems that he does not entirely evade symbolic castration, insofar as he does develop a certain but limited command over signs. By the end of Truffaut's film, Victor has learnt

16 For Lacan, the subject must "*refind* the object, whose emergence is fundamentally hallucinated." *The Seminar of Jacques Lacan Book III: The Psychoses 1955–1956*, trans. Russell Grigg (W.W. Norton & Company, 1997), 85.

17 See Peter Buse, "The Dog and the Parakeet: Lacan Among the Animals," *Angelaki* 22, no. 6 (2017): 133–45; and Zeynep Direk, "Animality in Lacan and Derrida: The Deconstruction of the Other" *SOPHIA* 57, no. 1 (2018): 21–37.

how to request milk by spelling the word "*lait*" with a set of wooden letters. Victor therefore at least becomes familiar or acquainted with the rules of symbolic exchange, even if he never demonstrates the requisite command over signs that would enable him speech.

The question of Victor's subjectivity is explicitly posed in the film's final ten minutes. Most of *L'Enfant sauvage*'s final act is devoted to a series of scenes in which Itard subjects Victor to a regime of tests and puzzles designed to improve his perceptual and linguistic abilities. This training progresses to the extent that eventually Victor is able to retrieve household items when Itard points to or proclaims their names. In one particular scene, Itard frets that Victor fails to understand the substance of his learning. The worry is that the boy understands the significance of what he is learning only insofar as it pertains to the dynamic between himself and Itard. "He only obeys me and corrects himself out of fear or hope of reward," says Itard: that is, Victor fails to grasp what he is learning from a meta or extra-contextual point of view. This doubt leads Itard to devise a test that aims, in effect, to detect whether Victor has recourse to "a virtual point of reference." Thus, Itard comes to the following idea: "I will test Victor's heart with a flagrant piece of injustice, by punishing him for no reason after he has succeeded before my eyes. I shall administer a punishment as odious as it is unjust precisely to see if his reaction is one of rebellion."

Itard acts on his word and punishes Victor for retrieving the objects that he had requested. Victor proceeds to rebel. After calming the agitated boy, Itard launches into an ecstatic internal monologue:

> I wish that my pupil could have understood me at that moment. I would have told him that his bite filled my soul with joy. How could I rejoice half-heartedly? I had

> evidence that what is just and unjust was no longer alien to Victor's heart. By provoking the sentiment, I had elevated the savage man to the stature of a moral being by the most noble of his attributes.

These sappy thoughts should sound suspicious. "I had elevated the savage man to the stature of a moral being . . ." Are these not the words of a man with a saviour complex? Indeed, Itard is a bit too excited by the prospect of glory in this moment to reflect on what has just happened with a sober mind. Was his experiment all that conclusive? Let's consider an alternate explanation: Victor protested Itard's punishment simply because his expectation of reward was frustrated. This expectation is written into the gleeful expression that Victor wears when he retrieves the correct items for Itard. That he rebelled does not necessarily indicate that Victor made a moral evaluation of the situation. On the contrary, his protest can be read as a simple sign of frustration.

While Victor does submit to Itard, he does so for instrumental reasons. He learns to submit because doing so has proved to serve his own interests. This leaves Itard with scant legitimation of his authority. An ordinary pupil would—at least hypothetically—recognise that Itard stands in a position of power over them because he has more knowledge than they do. But it is not clear that Victor perceives the epistemic inequality which, in principle, legitimates the authority that Itard wields. For Victor to be capable of this comparative judgement, he would have to have recourse to a virtual point of reference, an extra-contextual perspective. That he does not is evident insofar as Itard never inspires fear or idealisation in Victor. Which is to say that Victor perceives Itard "blankly." Victor's perception lacks the distortion that would make Itard appear *as* an authority, that is, *as* an other an other who knows "what the Big Other knows." That no repressed material mediates Victor's perception of Itard thus indicates that he has not undergone symbolic castration (or "primal repression" in Freud's language).[18]

On the contrary, it is Itard who demonstrates an idealised perception of Victor. Consider the final sequence of events in the film. Victor has legged it to live on the lam. After a few days, he returns to Itard's house of his own volition. Instead of welcoming him home with open arms, Itard scrambles to secure Victor by clasping him around the shoulders and escorting him indoors, where Mme Guérin envelops Victor in an embrace. After Guérin and Victor finish exchanging affections, Itard pulls Victor aside for another highfalutin monologue:

> I'm glad that you came home. Do you understand? This is your home. You're no longer a savage, even if you're not yet a man. Victor, you're an extraordinary young man. A young man of great expectations. Mme Guérin, take him up to rest.

With these words, Itard re-invests in his phantasmatic attachment to Victor—notably, with his proclamation that Victor is a young man "des grandes espérances" ("of great expectations"). Of course, Itard is really talking about his own "great expectations." For Itard, Victor represents the "great hope" that his decision to break from the opinion of his senior colleagues (who diagnosed the boy an idiot unfit for education) was not mere foolhardiness. The boy appears to Itard as a means for realising his greatest phantasy: to bring Victor the salvation of speech, and thereby to live on as a name responsible for a miraculous breakthrough in history and science.

---

18 Sigmund Freud, *Essays and Papers*, trans. Joan Riviere (Riverrun Editions, 2020), 294–97; see also Russell Grigg, *Lacan, Language and Philosophy* (State University of New York Press, 2008), 4.

Yet this phantasy is undercut by the film's final shot. Mme Guérin escorts Victor upstairs to get some rest. Itard calls out from the bottom of the stairwell, "later we'll resume our lessons." The camera cuts to Victor's reaction: he looks down at Itard with a scowl. An iris-in occludes everything except this severe expression. *Fin.* Victor's severe expression here exposes the emptiness of Itard's idealistic words. In effect, we are told that nothing more will come of these lessons: Victor has already reached his limit.

This last proposition is precisely what Itard must repress. In order to sustain his phantasy, he must go on believing that the limit of Victor's intelligence is yet to be determined, that education may still prove capable of bringing the young savage into the fold of a human society mediated by the universality of language. Along these lines, we might read the closing shot as taking place from Itard's perspective. The iris-in signifies the censor of his consciousness shutting itself off from the objectionable ideational content latent in Victor's scornful expression. However, this interpretation could only be sustained if the iris-in was inverted. The occlusion would have to—like a John Baldessari painting—begin by censoring Victor's expression. Instead, the occlusion works the other way. The iris-in highlights Victor's expression and solicits our sympathy for him. We are not in Itard's shoes, but Truffaut's. The final camera action thus separates Truffaut from his role as Itard and re-articulates his position behind the camera.

Truffaut ends the film by returning focus to sympathy for Victor. With this pivot, Truffaut distances himself from Itard by drawing the latter's phantasy of playing the benevolent father to a close. No *deus ex machina* will arrive to bestow Victor with the gift of speech and raise Itard to the dignity of a saviour. Instead, Victor's ascent of the staircase raises him beyond the reach of Itard's phantasy. Ushering him along, Mme Guérin leads Victor toward a future in her care, while Itard is left at a standstill. In this final moment, Truffaut forms a coalition between himself, Guérin, Victor, and the viewer, against Itard: the boy commands our sympathy precisely because he frustrates Itard's expectations. In the end, unification is wrought by silence, not speech.

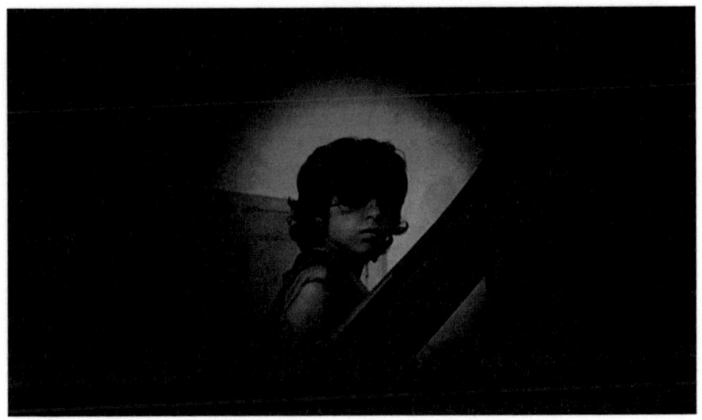

Philippa Hawker

Anybody Can Be Somebody: *Les Idoles* (1968)

I became curious about Les idoles *after learning that a minute of its footage appeared in the newly restored version of a work I have long been obsessed with, Jean Eustache's* La Maman et la putain *(1973). Once I saw* Les Idoles *and began to explore its background, it became another obsession, a portal into a rarely glimpsed, disappearing world of the avant-garde and 1960s culture, of performance, pop life, political critique, artistic collaboration, idealism, and wild style.*

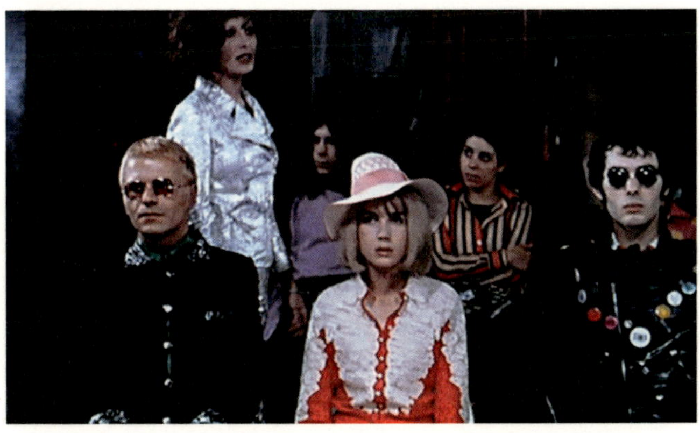

Les Idoles: Jean-Pierre Kalfon, Valérie Lagrange, Bulle Ogier, Pierre Clémenti (l to r)

1

Les Idoles, written and directed by Marc'o, occupies a small but significant place in the story of French cinema.[1] It stands at the intersection of the worlds of experimental theatre and film, and features some of France's most interesting actors and directors at early stages of their careers, including Bulle Ogier, Pierre Clémenti, Jean-Pierre Kalfon, Jean Eustache, and André Téchiné. It was barely seen at the time and is still rarely screened, yet its reputation has grown, its cultural prescience has become more apparent, and its vividness and swagger are as engaging as ever.

This tale of three pop stars—played by Clémenti, Kalfon and Ogier—is a mixture of the cautionary, the aleatory, and the exploratory. It's a hybrid, a self-aware musical that works on multiple levels; in telling the story of the stars, it takes us behind the scenes of a music business enterprise, examining the machinery that controls and exploits performers and manipulates the fans who consume what the performers produce. It is also an attractive object in its own right, a bright, shiny, and colourful pop confection that revels in its energies and absurdities and allows its actors a kind of delirious free rein. *Les Idoles* is an exhilarating affirmation of the work and nature of performance.

Les Idoles was a theatre piece before it was a movie, and it meant something very specific to those who were involved in its creation. In his 1973 memoir *Quelques messages personnels*, Clémenti writes that "it was definitely a satire of the world of show business, of the yé-ye wave, of the ideology and mythology of *Salut les copains*"—an immensely popular radio show and magazine that promoted pop music—"but it was also a

1 Marc'o and Marc'O seemed to be used interchangeably. I have chosen to use Marc'o, in accordance with the credits of *Les Idoles*. I have used a capital I for Idol when it refers to the characters Charly, Gigi, and Simon.

piece about us, about the crucial moment that we were at in our lives, a prefiguring of the breakup of our group."[2]

2

At the centre of this group is Marc'o, born Marc-Gilbert Guillaumin in Clermont-Ferrand in 1927, a fascinating, underappreciated figure in the worlds of theatre, cinema, and activism for more than seven decades. During World War II he fought with the Resistance; by 1950 he was organising poetry events with legendary writer Boris Vian at a venue called the Tabou. He became involved in the fledgling Lettrist movement that developed out of Dada and surrealism. "[Marc'o] was one of the youngest members of the Lettrist movement but he was physically tough and obdurate; he had been a *résistant* and *maquisard*, fighting undercover in the *maquis*, the harsh countryside of the Auvergne, and had been seriously injured there in a shootout with the Germans," writes Andrew Hussey in his biography of avant-garde filmmaker Isidore Isou, one of Marc'o's close associates in his early years.[3]

Marc'o was the first to publish Guy Debord, in a one-off cinema manifesto, *Ion*.[4] He produced several films within this avant-garde milieu, including Isou's *Traité de bavé et d'éternité* (*Treatise on Venom and Eternity*, 1951). The first film he directed, *Closed Vision*, a cinematic stream of consciousness (tagline: "Sixty minutes in the interior life of a man"), screened at Cannes in 1954. He had inventive and radical notions for cinema, for its production, exhibition, and reception. In his essay in *Ion*, his focus was very much on the spectator or "the receiving element," suggesting that the situation of the audience

2 Pierre Clémenti, *Quelques messages personnels* (Éditions Gallimard, 2005), 91.

3 Andrew Hussey, *Speaking East: The Strange and Enchanted Life of Isidore Isou* (Reaktion Books, 2021), 212.

4 *Ion: Centre de création*, no. 1 (1952), ed. Marc-Gilbert Guillaumin.

and the physical conditions of the cinema space are vital to the experience and reality of a film.[5]

In the 1960s, Marc'o gravitated towards the stage, a decision driven by his desire to explore the nature of performance. He emphasised the actor as a creative figure, making a conscious shift away from the traditional French focus on the text. He was interested in a particular kind of immersive, improvisational approach, and in the work of companies such as New York's Living Theater. He established the Centre for Theatre and Experimentation in Performance, working for a time at the American Center at 261 Boulevard Raspail, a key site for experimental artists in the 1960s. "It became a theatre laboratory," Marc'o recalled in *Libération* in 2004, "and I established a group of young actors who followed me in this adventure. I wrote pieces for them."[6]

3

A side note, but an intriguing one to me: among Marc'o's Paris colleagues was Keith Humble, an Australian composer, musician, and teacher who left his homeland in the early 1960s, setting up his Centre de Musique at the American Center and turning it into a force in contemporary music. Humble was involved as musical director in early Marc'o projects, stagings of Glück's *L'ivrogne corrigé* and Schönberg's *Pierrot Lunaire*, and he composed the music for an original Marc'o work, *Le printemps*, which featured Ogier and Clémenti. He returned to Australia in the mid-'60s, where he became an influential composer and teacher. He is said to have drawn inspiration for his theories

5 Marc'o, "Cinéma Nucléaire ou l'École Oienne du Cinéma," in *Ion: Centre de création,* no. 1 (1952). Republished by Jean-Paul Rocher (1999): 253–84.

6 Marc'o, "Mes dates-clés par Marc'O," *Libération*, 16 June 2004. Here, as throughout, the translations from French are my own unless indicated otherwise.

about improvisation in part from Marc'o's approach. What Humble learned and applied to his own musical practice, wrote John Whiteoak in 1989, is that "through repeated improvisations, intuitive group response will eventually draw more or less random elements together to define structure."[7] Humble is one of many creative figures to have clarified their practice through working with Marc'o.

4

The pop or yé-yé milieu might seem at first glance an unlikely setting for an experimental theatre group, but according to André Téchiné, writing in 1967 in *Cahiers du cinéma*, "Marc'o chose the world of yé-yé because in his eyes it remains the only living form in which the audience plays a real role."[8] It fitted perfectly, in other words, with his theories about the significance of the spectator in the creative process.

Marc'o began writing *Les Idoles* in 1964; it was first staged two years later, in a printing workshop specially converted into a performance space for the production. A contemporary review described the setup: "The stage is a boxing ring. The walls are covered in posters. Spectators come and go. Theatrical conventions are abandoned. Actors and musicians mingle with audience members, who look just like them: long hair and short skirts, young women and young men with beautiful faces, androgynous, free, and pure."[9] Spectators were given glasses of red wine before the show—they couldn't afford

7 John Whiteoak, "Interview with Keith Humble," *NMA 7* (1989), republished on rainerlinz.net.

8 André Téchiné, "Les Idoles: du Bilboquet au cinema," *Cahiers du cinéma* no. 191 (June 1967): 7.

9 An image showing part of a contemporary newspaper review appears in the short film *À rebours, Les Idoles* (2016), an extra on the DVD release of *Les Idoles* (Park City Films, 2016). No bibliographic information is provided.

champagne, Ogier recalls in her 2019 memoir *J'ai oublié*—and on Fridays, there were two free tickets for any spectator who entered the theatre on a motorbike.[10] It was part theatre piece, part musical, part happening. Marc'o encouraged over-the-top performances, Kalfon writes in his 2018 memoir *Tout va bien m'man!*, and audiences could get turbulent.[11] On one chaotic night, he recalls, when audience members were whistling and hurling insults, he wondered if they were disgruntled yé-yé fans who thought their stars were being mocked.

In fact, Kalfon says, whatever resemblances to reality that spectators and reviewers might perceive, *Les Idoles* "wasn't about imitating or critiquing existing singers" but rather about "depicting their exploitation by a system that, after having allowed them to rise, to a degree, then threw them away like used Kleenex."[12]

A second season was presented in a bigger venue. According to Clémenti, everyone in the cultural and arts scene in Paris came to the show. It attracted high-profile spectators, with regulars including Jean Genet, Guy Debord, Jean-Jacques Lebel, and Rudolf Nureyev. And producers were circling. Ironically, some of them envisaged a pop future for the cast, Clémenti told *Les Inrockuptibles* in a 1998 interview.[13] He was the last person who would have been interested in this. "In playing idols, we refused to become them, even if we were seen that way to some extent by the fringe audience of the café-theatres," he wrote in his memoir. "But that was nothing compared to how the industry wanted to exploit us."[14]

10 Bulle Ogier with Anne Diatkine, *J'ai oublié* (Éditions du Seuil, 2019), 47.

11 Jean-Pierre Kalfon, *Tout va bien, M'man!* (Éditions de l'archipel, 2018), 138.

12 Ibid., 137.

13 Clémenti, "Pierre Clémenti: La voie lactée", interview with *Les Inrockuptibles*, 18 March 1998.

14 Clémenti, *Quelques messages personnels*, 93.

5

Marc'o found backers for a screen version that was shot in 1967. The film retains some of the framing of the theatrical work, beginning with a scene involving an audience of press and fans summoned to an "Ask Me Anything" session with the three Idols. Over the course of the film, we learn about the manipulations and machinations of what I will call the Idol Project, whose influence extends far beyond the music business. But at this stage, the spotlight is on the stars, who arrive wearing towelling robes over their outfits like boxers before a fight, as they are mobbed by an enthusiastic crowd. The event is mediated by PR representatives, with a backing band that sings introductory numbers about each star. The occasion is meant to launch them as a supergroup trio, but it turns out that the Idols themselves have other plans. They sing trademark songs, but as they begin to tell the story of their lives, another narrative is unfolding, a story of resistance and escape.

It is not surprising, given Marc'o's focus on actors, that they are the most striking feature of *Les Idoles*. They give us a series of explorations of the presented self, of the performed identity of each Idol, alongside a yearning for something beyond appearance. There's a ferocious commitment to the songs in all their variety, and to every aspect of the work of performance.

For Nicole Brenez, a critic who has written extensively on Marc'o and on experimental cinema, it is important to note that "we're still moved by *Les Idoles* because, far from unilaterally criticising popular singers, it presents them as incorruptible figures, deeply idealistic and sincere, and it acknowledges their physical energy via an inventiveness—in body language, vocal delivery, and facial expression—that makes the film a deceptively iconoclastic and authentically celebratory work.

Les Idoles is above all a striking tribute to the actor's practice as a guarantee of access to the truth."[15]

6

When the Idols are presented to the studio audience, we are introduced first to Clémenti's character Charly le Surineur ("Charly the Knife"), a brooding bad boy in a leather jacket who is reminiscent of 1960s stars such as Johnny Hallyday. Charly has a sinuous swagger, a lip curled in contempt, but Clémenti also brings a fluid, Dionysian abandon to this role of a street hoodlum turned Idol. Clémenti as Charly maintains a degree of detachment from his fame and his audience, and can project the dandy as well as the delinquent.

Clémenti himself had a tough childhood, but a stint in an institution—which he compares to the reform school in Truffaut's *Les Quatre Cents Coups* (*The 400 Blows*, 1959)—also brought him in contact with a teacher who encouraged pupils to read and learn poetry.[16] He became determined to pursue an acting career, despite multiple obstacles. He made his first film in 1960—he was considered French cinema's go-to delinquent, he says in his interview with *Les Inrockuptibles*—but he was always interested in experimental work, in pushing the boundaries of art and performance.[17] When he heard about Marc'o's theatre group, he went to see a rehearsal of *Le printemps* with Bulle Ogier, and was immediately on board. In *Quelques messages personnels*, Clémenti writes with feeling about the experience of working with the troupe, the immediacy of performance, exploring new ideas, testing them in front of an

15 Nicole Brenez, "Autour des Idoles, Jalons pour une histoire du cinéma élargie". In *Le Préjugé de la Rampe, pour un cinéma déchaîné,* ed. Bernard Benolie (ACOR 2004), 33.

16 Clémenti, "La voie lactée."

17 Ibid.

audience, and feeling a sense of community and collaboration, without thought of career or personal advancement.[18]

7

We then meet Gigi la Folle ("Crazy Gigi"), Ogier's character. Gigi is ambitious and hustling, determined to make it as an Idol; her mod-pop princess look suggests a number of stars of the period, including Sylvie Vartan, a singer married for some time to Hallyday. Ogier describes Gigi's hairstyle as "half Brian Jones, half France Gall," and calls the character "brazen and extrovert[ed]." Ogier has a gleeful, capering energy; Adrian Martin, writing appreciatively about *Les Idoles* in *The Little Black Book: Movies* (2007), notes that she "channels the yé-yé pop starlet phenomenon into something magnificently monstrous."[19]

Unlike Clémenti and Kalfon, Ogier came to acting more by chance rather than by desire. In *J'ai oublié*, she describes how she was drawn into the world of theatre and performance; she was in a relationship with Marc'o, who suggested to her one day that she might like to step onto the stage, that it could do her good.[20]

Marguerite Duras—who directed Ogier in films and plays—is often quoted as saying: "Bulle ce n'est pas la nouvelle vague, c'est le vague absolu" ("Bulle is not the new wave; Bulle is absolute vagueness"), a punning appreciation of her elusive, evanescent quality as an actor. In her memoir, Ogier cites this remark, and Marc'o's equally playful response: "Pas du tout! Bulle, c'est une lame de fond!" ("Not at all! Bulle is a tidal wave!")[21]

---

18 Clémenti, *Quelques messages personnels*, 90.

19 Adrian Martin, "Key person, Gigi la Folle, Bulle Ogier, Les Idoles," in *The Little Black Book: Movies*, ed. Chris Fujiwara (Cassell, 2007), 415.

20 Ogier, *J'ai oublié*, 22.

21 Ibid., 11–12.

8

The third Idol is Simon Le Magicien, played by Kalfon. With his platinum hair and empathetic, mystical vibe, he has no obvious yé-yé reference point. His career is more volatile than that of the others, and he is both philosophical and strategic about resurrecting it. Before he was an Idol, we learn, Simon was a clairvoyant specialising in telling the future by "reading" the smell of a broken egg. He can be melancholy and introspective, but has unexpected bursts of energy. There is a wild, Jerry Lewis-style physical improvisation in Kalfon's performance as Simon—an unpredictable highlight of the stage show for Kalfon that proved harder for him to nail on set.

Kalfon's parents hoped he would be a doctor or a lawyer; instead he ran away from home at fifteen and spent two years in Belgium before returning to Paris. His first job as a performer was with the Folies Bergère, followed by a drama course and an immersion in the theatre scene. In 1959, he made his film debut. He and Clémenti moved in the same circles: Kalfon gave Clémenti his first role on stage, and Clémenti introduced Kalfon to Marc'o and his troupe. Kalfon was the only one of the three leads already involved in playing music; as well as his extensive theatre and film work, he continued along this musical path his whole life.

Kalfon sees the Idols as precursors as well as emblems of their time. "Our characters," he suggests, "are instinctive protesters [...] You can see it in how we sing and move, above all in the way we take provocation as far as it can go. The English and the Americans say they invented punk, but really Bulle Ogier and Pierre Clémenti and me, we were pre-punks!"[22]

22 Jean-Pierre Kalfon, "Rencontre avec Jean-Pierre Kalfon," interview by Victorien Dauoût. In *Culture aux trousses*, January 16, 2019.

9

Much of the film was shot in the performance space where *Les Idoles* was first presented, but Marc'o also brought in architect Claude Parent and cultural theorist Paul Virilio as consultants to source interesting locations and interiors, such as hip contemporary houses and office spaces, a multi-level garden setting, and a desolate urban maze. Jean Bouquin, a fashion designer famous for dressing Brigitte Bardot, was the film's costume designer. He had already worked for free on the stage version, and he had encouraged actors to source parts of their outfits from flea markets. Memorable wardrobe decisions range from Kalfon's spectacular jacket with screen-printed images of JFK, to Ogier's see-through plastic coat over white lingerie, to Clémenti's variations on black leather, augmented by a large rubber spider on a chain around his neck.

The costumes—from Charly's American flag shirt to the Idols' red-white-and-blue outfits to the JFK jacket—also gesture towards the political and nationalist resonances of the Idol Project, an aspect referenced in various ways, from a song about France's national day, the 14th of July, to a number listing the precise amount of the Idol Project's financial support for Defence Department initiatives.

10

Les Idoles doesn't allow itself to be easily categorised or pinned down. There is an exuberant, episodic quality to the film, an embrace of abrupt transitions, sudden shifts in tone and scrambled time frames. Gary Indiana, in a 2005 profile of Ogier, describes how it "mixes artificial and natural spaces, interrupting filmic and theatrical modes of reception. An action that starts in one place continues in a different one, often in mid-dialogue."[23] The songs—written by Marc'o with house band the Les Rollsticks—are not only pop numbers, but also narrative devices and expressions of the self, unexpected affirmations of alternative possibilities or versions of events. This deliberately chaotic presentation serves to complicate any sense of a fixed reality, of how to read what is happening in front of us.

11

The theme of manipulation runs through *Les Idoles.* There are times when this is transparent, when the managers and PR people are happy to acknowledge and promote their construction of the Idol persona. Press attaché Jean Camel, introducing Charly to a crowd of stakeholders, announces that this new Idol is "the living proof that anybody can be somebody, [therefore] if anybody can be somebody, as soon as he's somebody, he's no longer anybody!" This phrase echoes a moment in the Canadian documentary short *Lonely Boy* (1962), directed by Wolf Koenig and Roman Kroitor, which lays bare the tightly controlled life of teenage singing star Paul Anka, whose manager tells him, "You no longer belong to yourself, you belong to the world."

This scene also contains an intriguing moment of connection between the Idols, a foreshadowing of what is to come. As Camel proclaims that an Idol "must behave and talk like anyone would expect him to [...] an Idol always does what the public expect him to do," there are two close-ups, one after the other. The first is of a reflective Gigi, sitting in the audience, half-closing her eyes and giving a slight smile; the second is of Charly, lifting his head a little, keeping his eyes lowered, then blinking and looking sideways. In the midst of a scene that's all about

23 Gary Indiana, "Daughter of the Revolution," *Film Comment* 41, no. 2 (March-April 2005), 47.

control, strategy, and the Idol as an object, this juxtaposition brings the pair together in a kind of shared interiority.

12

The relationship between stars and fans is presented by the Idol Project as a natural, inevitable form of engagement. "I love the audience because they love me," Gigi tells an interviewer at the beginning of the film. But it's a conditional relationship with many layers to it. The film contains a shrewd account of fandom as a powerful force, managed and manipulated but also capricious and ungovernable, hard to ignore or predict, with its own fierce momentum. The most notable example comes from the depiction of a young woman called La Nyasse, Simon's most ardent fan, whose attitude towards him shifts from faithful to fickle to fatal. By the end, it seems, she is prepared to kill the thing she loves.

13

Les Idoles shows the operation of an enterprise that extends beyond the music industry into the media, the church, and political institutions, promoting by stealth everything from conservative family values to national identity.

Yet, paradoxically, to maintain the Idols, the product needs to keep changing. The PR department decides that Charly and Gigi will get married, as a way to boost lagging record sales. The pair make it clear that they don't have any feelings for each other, but the wedding juggernaut is unstoppable. A wedding ceremony is staged. The press happily buys into the charade because it will make them money; the institution of the church, represented by the officiating priest, Abbé Vincent—played by avant-garde artist and actor Daniel Pommereulle—blesses the marriage, with the warning that popular music must "stay within the bounds of decency, of healthy pleasure, respectable distraction." Bernadette Lafont, an actor who was close to several of the Marc'o troupe, has a cameo role at the wedding; her character, Soeur Hilarité, clearly references a genuine 1960s pop phenomenon, Soeur Sourire, also known as the Singing Nun. Lafont's presence is broadly comic and tongue-in-cheek, as she sings her new hit for the supposedly happy couple.

It all blows up, however, at the PR event, when Charly responds to a question about compulsory military service by saying that he won't do it. There is immediate public outrage, fuelled by the media. The PR team goes into overdrive, but they have increasing difficulty controlling the narrative. And the Idols themselves are no longer prepared to play the game in quite the same way. Their concerns—for each other, and for the absurdity and impossibility of their position—are evident. They are not what their masters wish them to be. The film's ending is sudden and ambiguous, but also resonant. It works on multiple levels, as its central characters both succumb to and transcend their fates.

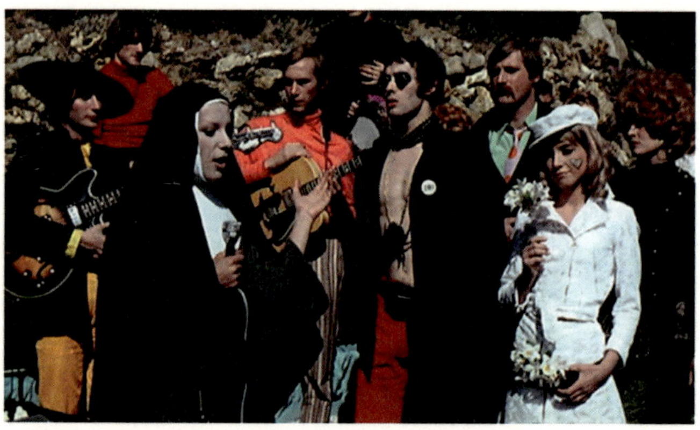

Bernadette Lafont, Pierre Clémenti, Bulle Ogier (l to r)

14

The release of *Les Idoles* was delayed until 1968, and as social and political upheaval brought France to a standstill that year, Marc'o decided to withdraw the film, feeling that there were more pressing issues at hand. Many of the cast and crew would work together again, but the life of the company had come to an end. In mid-1968, Marc'o realised that he no longer wanted to make theatre in France. He went to Italy, deciding to dedicate himself to more overt political activism.

The theatrical version of *Les Idoles* had already made an impact on the cinematic lives of many of its actors. Jacques Rivette acknowledged how impressed he was by the extraordinary work of this theatre group. He cast Kalfon and Ogier in his monumental *L'Amour fou* (shot in 1967, the same year as *Les Idoles*, but not released until 1969). This story of a theatre production and a complicated play of relationships within the company, Rivette freely acknowledged, was inspired by Marc'o and his troupe: "The film was marked by what I was discovering at the time in the theatre, namely the performances of Marc'o, and his actors."[24]

Working on the film version of *Les Idoles* also had an impact on crew members, including Jean Eustache, who was an editor, and André Téchiné, who was an assistant director. Eustache said in an interview in 1971 with *La Revue du cinéma* that the experience of watching Marc'o at work was a formative one, which changed his notion of collaboration: "Before, I thought that the director should absolutely control everything, that he should be the absolute master [...] Since then, thanks to Marc'o, I've realised that Renoir was right in what he said and always practised, namely that you have to let yourself be devoured, absorbed by the actors, which seems

24 Jacques Rivette, "Entretien: Jacques Rivette," interview with *Les Inrockuptibles*, 19 March 2007.

really obvious, but also by the whole crew, and then to digest everything and reconstruct it."[25]

15

Since its brief initial release, *Les Idoles* has made sporadic appearances in cinemas and on screens. It had a theatrical re-release in France in 1973 and 2004. In 2006, it was broadcast on French television in a rock opera marathon alongside *Pink Floyd: The Wall* (Alan Parker, 1982), *Purple Rain* (Albert Magnoli, 1984), *Tommy* (Ken Russell, 1975), and *Velvet Goldmine* (Todd Haynes, 1998). It was part of a "French New Wave Turns 50" retrospective in Australia in 2007 at Brisbane's Gallery of Modern Art, and it had its US premiere in 2008 at the Lincoln Center in New York, followed by a yé-yé afterparty. In 2016, a restored, unsubtitled version came out on DVD in France.

It's possible to see *Les Idoles* as a piece of cinematic pop deconstruction that exists in a line running from Godard's *Masculin féminin* (1966) to Harry Elfont and Deborah Kaplan's *Josie and the Pussycats* (2001), sharing elements of Richard Lester's *A Hard Day's Night* (1964), Peter Watkins' *Privilege* (1967), and Bob Rafelson's *Head* (1968).

But it has other resonances too. For Clémenti, *Les Idoles* was an important work that "recorded the atmosphere of the era, the spirit of the times. The other two great films of this period are Rivette's *L'Amour fou* and Eustache's *La Maman et la putain*," he told *Les Inrockuptibles*.[26]

Eustache incorporated footage from *Les Idoles* in the first release of *La Maman et la putain*, which had its controversial premiere at Cannes in 1973. This segment was later cut, and

25 Jean Eustache, "Entretien avec Jean Eustache," interview by Philippe Haudique. *La Revue du cinéma, image et son* no. 250 (May 1971): 86.

26 Clémenti, "La voie lactée."

has only just been reinstated in the long-awaited restoration that was screened at Cannes in 2022. In this version, about two-thirds of the way through, two of the main characters, Alexandre (Jean-Pierre Léaud) and Marie (Bernadette Lafont), are at the movies together, and we see brief clips of what they are watching. This footage is shown in black and white in keeping with the format of Eustache's film. The work they are watching is not identified, however; what is shown, fleetingly, are images in the aftermath of Charly and Gigi's sham wedding that, out of context, suggest a kind of psychedelic sexual trauma. In between these brief extracts, we see Alexandre and Marie, sitting in the cinema, holding hands and exchanging a smile.

It is not clear why Eustache chose to reference *Les Idoles* in *La Maman et la putain*, even if he and Lafont were both connected to it, and it is not clear why he chose this particular footage. Film historian Vincent Lowy, who worked on the restoration, noted in an interview with the broadcaster *France Culture* that Eustache, just before his death in 1981, had told his son, Boris, to cut this material. Lowy had reservations about its re-inclusion for various reasons, feeling that it detracted from *La Maman et la putain*: "It brings something trivial to a film that is anything but trivial. And something of its time to a film that is timeless," he said.[27] But the clip had been part of the original feature for some nine years, and the decision was therefore made to bring it back.

Lowy's characterisation feels like an odd way to describe the clip and its place in the world of Eustache's film: part of the timelessness of *La Maman et la putain* is its complex mixture of anachronism and topicality, and the little in-jokes that he includes about films that his actors have made. So there

27 Vincent Lowy, "'La Maman et la putain': une restauration 'magnifique' pour 'un film totalement inactuel et intemporel'," interview by Éric Chaverou, *France Culture*, June 2, 2022.

it is, an Eustachean Easter egg, an entry point, the return of a once-forgotten film inside a film that was for many years elusive and hard to find.

After *Les Idoles*, Marc'o, Pierre Clémenti, Bulle Ogier, and Jean-Pierre Kalfon went in different directions, but their paths often intersected and they remained close. Clémenti died in 1999, but now, at the time of writing, Ogier and Kalfon are still alive. In their memoirs, all three actors recall in different yet complementary ways the work they did with Marc'o and on *Les Idoles*. It was clearly a potent, memorable, vital experience.

Marc'o died in Paris in June 2025, at the age of 98, after a long life of creativity, activism, influence, and unpredictability. I would like to imagine that, like me, more people will discover not only *Les Idoles*, but also the world, the vision, and the creative collaborations that Marc'o brought into being.

Scott Robinson

Tourists of a Sentimental History: *Visages Villages* (2017)

> *We have given up one portion of the human heritage after another, and have often left it at the pawnbrokers for a hundredth of its true value, in exchange for the small change of "the contemporary."*
>
> Walter Benjamin, "Experience and Poverty"

In a small, verdant cemetery in the south of France, Agnès Varda and JR visit the grave of Henri Cartier-Bresson. Like his wife Martine Franck's next to his, the length of the grave sprouts picturesque lavender and the tomb is studded with stones, to which Varda adds one for each grave. JR remembers one of Cartier-Bresson's famous images, while Varda remarks that the expression "the decisive moment" was not one he liked. They wander off. Then, perched on a wall, they realise they have not taken any photographs. JR takes the opportunity to casually ask Varda if she is afraid of death. They snap some tokens of their visit as Varda reflects on mortality. As the narrator recites in Varda's early travelogue *Du côté de la côte* (*Along the Coast*, 1958), "Because they cannot own a Matisse, they come to see his tomb."

Varda's own mortality provides a thematic device to structure the loosely connected scenes in the 2017 co-production *Visages Villages.* The ageing body becomes a central motif of the film, often focused on Varda herself and specifically her eyes. These touching vignettes are nestled in the picturesque landscapes of the French countryside and bathed in a generational memorialisation. The glow of history in the sunny film palette signifies the sunset of one generation, and a sunrise for another more mercenary art that will step in to make use of the images left behind. JR's whole practice enfolds, layer by layer, the merciless appropriation of images, shifting seamlessly from hyper-local yet monumental portraits to global social media platforms. Likewise, his image-making practice implants itself parasitically within Varda's film practice: his team swoop into scenes to paste images on walls, and his "Inside Outside Photo Truck"™ churns out smiling, oversized portraits with the cheap nostalgia of a Polaroid camera. The film's weak narrative drive manages to suggest the passing of one generation of filmmakers associated with the *nouvelle vague*, and with them a shift in modes of image-making. Both of these solemn valedictions are, by less-than-subtle insinuation, meant to pass the credentials of luminaries such as Varda onto charlatans like JR.

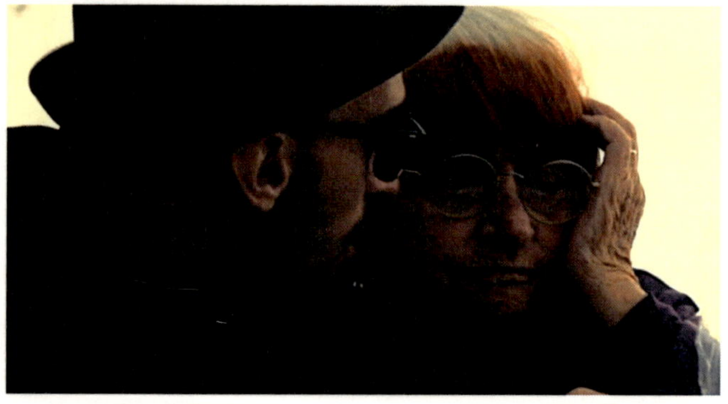

The meeting and occasion for the film is orchestrated by a series of missed meet-cutes, suggesting that Varda and JR occupy the same world, walk the same routes, take the same buses, and yet do not notice one another. Instead, they see each other's images, with JR's media-friendly installations placed in montage alongside images culled from Varda's historically significant oeuvre. This comparison should alert us to the stakes of the film, and to the sleight of hand with which it assimilates the pasted silo art of JR's social media fame to Varda's position as what Richard Neupert calls the "most significant woman filmmaker of the past fifty years."[1] While it serves as a charming, quirky introduction to Varda's film history, this presentation of her work constantly places it in a context that JR can claim, and one that frames French history in rosy terms. The composition of images is sutured to a picturesque conception of the French economy. The prominent features of the economy include chemical manufacturing, agriculture, and tourism. These features are framed without conflict, in ways that run counter to the long-standing concerns of Varda's filmmaking.

In early films such as the wittily ironic *Du côté de la côte*, the brilliant, unorthodox study of image-making and ethnography *Daguerréotypes* (1975), or the complex narrative of dissonance in the feminist movement in *L'une chante, l'autre pas* (*One Sings, the Other Doesn't*, 1977), Varda's images infused their charm and beauty with tension—just as, in *Sans toit ni loi* (*Vagabond*, 1985), Mona's resolute freedom is constantly endangered. *Visages Villages* dispenses with tension. It sentimentalises what in major works like *Les Glaneurs et la glaneuse* (*The Gleaners and I*, 2000) were the eruptions of a repressed history into the very landscape of agricultural production and even urban survival. Here, the countryside is transformed into a brochure, and the dilapidated and ddeindustrialised parts of France visited by JR and Varda are literally pasted with oversized portraits. Since

1 Richard Neupert, *A History of the French New Wave Cinema* (Madison: University of Wisconsin Press, 2007), 300.

its jubilant reception, significantly boosted by JR's self-promotion (both on social media and on his travels carrying a cutout of Varda's image), the film has received mostly hagiographic treatment. These responses propose a continuity between *Visages Villages* and the rest of Varda's work, reinterpreting her concerns in light of the later film. I argue that the film in fact contributes to obscuring and, worse, re-narrating her significance as a filmmaker in terms of a sentimental history.

Sentimentality takes up the slack of narrative movement or formal experiment in *Visages Villages*' treatment of film history, French industrial relations, and landscapes. Varda's playful techniques and explorations of the cinematic medium—from painting to postcard, grainy handheld first-person testimony to delicately framed landscapes—now come to serve the construction of a persona instead of the image. JR's frantic, industrialised image-making practice, tailored to the social media age, vampirically attaches itself to the persona of an ageing Varda. The film's availability for such treatment is demonstrated by its uptake towards the sort of "motivation and inspiration" characteristic of late capitalism's intensified demands for work on the self. "Varda was an artist, but she was also a businesswoman," asserts Kelley Conway.[2] Even the elderly cannot escape the injunction; Varda becomes a model for late-in-life self-realisation, as if her career were simply the material for this packaged summary of it. Acclaimed for its celebration of Varda herself, the film certainly makes abundant use of her work, but in ways that simplify and decontextualise its achievements. Its consistent use of tropes and references from Varda's work serves to tame, mute, and appropriate her cinematic voice to the end of JR's careerist ambitions. Praised for what Claudia Gorbman calls the constant "refining and maturation of

2 Kelley Conway, "Agnès Varda, Producer," *Camera Obscura* 36.1, no. 106 (2021): 109.

[Varda's] cinematic voice," *Visages Villages* makes for an awkward tribute.[3]

Along with the flimsy premise disguised by the opening sequence of missed meet-cutes, the most consistent thematic undertow in *Visages Villages* is the fading of Varda's vision. In literal terms, we witness JR's insistent manipulation of the techniques of image-making as he takes on the role of director in numerous scenes. He orchestrates the anonymous subjects of the films: the villagers assembled as decorative icons for oversized portraits produced to paste on their own village walls. In similar terms, with similar condescension, JR directs Varda herself as he photographs her feet, or spectularises her vision tests and exposed eyeball in a shot that reminds Varda of the notorious slicing in Luis Buñuel and Salvador Dalí's *Un chien andalou* (1929). Rebecca DeRoo has identified as distinctive of Varda's filmmaking the practice of intermixing mediums.[4] Yet in *Visages Villages*, despite the presence of another artist with an image-making practice of his own, Varda shows little interest. In films such as *Daguerréotypes*, the whole architecture and orchestration of image-production becomes thematically significant. Yet while displaying scaffolding and a busy production team, as well as travelling in a van mimicking a camera, here Varda's lack of interest seems to acknowledge the derivativeness and flattening effect of JR's photographic vision. Blinded by its charming sentimentality, we are invited to ignore distinctions. The sentimental approach to JR's images of opportunistic self-promotion invites us to accept them complacently, rather than as objects of contemplation or disruption more characteristic of Varda's filmmaking.

3 Claudia Gorbman, "Finding a Voice: Varda's Early Travelogues," *SubStance* 41, no. 2 (2012): 40.

4 Rebecca J. DeRoo, *Agnès Varda between Film, Photography and Art* (University of California Press, 2018), 170.

The film proceeds with its thinly connected itinerary through the French countryside, from a dour, de-industrialised north to a sunny, vibrant south. In each location, Varda and JR produce images often representing members of the town, village, or industrial site. The process of image-making in the villages corresponds to a paradigm of activation, bringing a community together through the act of representation, doing so by shedding the film of what Jacques Rancière calls the aesthetic image that would give it a power to disturb (and any potential of image-making to expose conflict, difference, or tension).[5] They collect, manage, and represent the community via monumentalised images of its photogenic members. The community is formed as a whole through the representative process, and similarly, the economic and social history that had occupied Varda's previous excursions to these sites is replaced with an historical narrative that imposes cohesion over disparate, even conflicting elements.

For example, an early trip finds JR and Varda in a small deindustrialised northern town, with rows of identical miners' houses slated for destruction. They fawn over the last remaining resident, and mingle with locals with whom Varda exchanges memories in the form of postcards. Postcards partly narrate the distance between two women's lives in *L'une chante, l'autre pas*, while they provide an ironic comment on the advertising image of the Riviera in *Du côté de la côte*. Here they serve to transform complex, ambivalent histories of coal mining in the region into a cute, safely distant past. The postcard, according to Naomi Schor, erases the context of image production and "wipes out both labour and history."[6] Here we are given a neatly packed dose of nostalgia that romanticises the working conditions of the miners and ignores

5 Jacques Rancière, *The Future of the Image*, trans. Gregory Elliott (Verso, 2007).

6 Naomi Schor, "'Cartes Postales': Representing Paris 1900," *Critical Inquiry* 18, no. 2 (1992): 201.

the displacements of deindustrialisation effected on the very houses upon which JR's team paste their images.

The postindustrial context also shapes the comparison set up in the film between two goat farmers. In *Les Glaneurs et la glaneuse*, Varda targets industrialised agriculture for practices of both waste and (cost and labour) efficiency that deny the poor the right to harvest surplus products. In *Visages Villages*, this problem is reduced to the goat's right to have horns. One farm dehorns its modest herd of goats; the other does not. While it retains the language of docility, productivity, and profitability that indicts the practice, the implied critique of industrial agriculture is blander in the later film. In the sentimental context of the film's softened approach to political and economic conditions, the implied critique is almost trivialised. The romanticised scene of the un-dehorned goats (a sort of double negative liberty) is concluded with their carefree owners running off to corral escaped goats from the road.

These scenes are connected with little narrative motivation. The journey from village to chemical factory is accomplished with little more than a series of picturesque landscapes, as if the scenery were airbrushed so that fields placidly gave way to factories nestled unproblematically in their folds. A meagre effort to situate the factory is accomplished by JR and Varda's subjection to an OHS video, whose abstract images of cascading piles of minerals and machinery could, in a different Varda film, incite visual humour or a surreal interlude. Instead, the disenchantment of the image is deepened by the friendly, consensual framing of relations within the factory.

JR and Varda's project in this setting takes the form of a group photo, which involves directing employees like schoolchildren into playful configurations. Like the workers themselves, the image is visibly treated as manipulable and docile. Moreover, like an exercise in team building, the images construct a fantasy of harmony between workers and management. Yet the context of France's political economy cannot completely disappear. One worker announces that he is taking early retirement: a cause for ambivalent celebration and apprehension for his "whole new life" set amid the background of the rising pension age. Another "character" sought by JR and Varda brushes over his small pension with a hippy stoicism of small needs that renders his dire economic situation a lifestyle choice we can affirm as a quirk. This vagabond bohemian is a safer, sunnier incarnation of a character in *Les Glaneurs et la glaneuse*, whose overflowing collection of toys, shaped crudely into sculptures, looms through a foreboding gloom while remaining sealed behind high walls.

The romance of poverty, like the romance of deindustrialisation, provides the occasion for JR to plaster the scenery with his projects. An unfinished seaside village, just a collection of prefabricated concrete walls languishing in a field, is introduced with swooping establishing shots worthy of a home renovation show. Towards the conclusion of the film, JR and Varda visit Le Havre, where JR bounces over the shipping containers before Varda takes the wives of some dock workers off to a field for a picnic and chat. Ignoring the fact that these wives turn out to be, themselves, workers (another context elided by the film), Varda schemes to literally totemise these women as props to their husbands' workplace, stacking pasted shipping containers to form enormous portraits in the dockyards.

In one of the final scenes, Varda talks with a trainyard worker about her and JR's project, as this man looks on, bemused, at train carriages bearing images of eyes and toes. By way of a post-hoc synthesis of the film's premise, she suggests that their project has been about "being with people at work." However, the people "at" work almost never appear working. Their work is rendered invisible by the gentrification of the workplace as a site of play or fun, concealing relations of production and whatever other context Varda might, in other films, have examined. This gentrification is consistent with JR's body of work, such as the monumental images he pasted in Rio de Janeiro's port zone, "whose recent revitalisation displaced thousands of people," according to Alexandra Pechman.[7] Even where the dockworkers' wives proclaim their unwavering support for the union, they bury their own politics and conditions of employment. *Visages Villages* neglects to interrogate the implicit gender politics at stake here.

The jolly tour of the French countryside gives *Visages Villages* the feel of a tourism promotion. Two of Varda's earliest and most delightful films—the 1957 commission *Ô saisons, ô châteaux* (1958), and *Du côté de la côte*—also have the quality of "travelogues," but they use this form to very different effect. As Claudia Gorbman notes in her account of these early films, Varda approaches the travelogue form with humour, and in the year that separates the first from the second, we find notable aesthetic developments in Varda's style.[8] Irony and wit saturate the later film, and while both remain steadfastly ludic, *Du côté de la côte* dwells on the privacy and pleasure purchased by wealthy visitors. In contrast, *Visages Villages* extols the sunny beauty of the French countryside, in each instance turning peopled and produced images into naturalised enticements to superficial enchantment.

JR and Varda lay siege to a series of villages in the south of France, their central squares appropriated for the spectacular projection of some local who stands in for the whole village. The bell ringer in one village tells a story of the transmission of his craft, before we follow him up the tower to the bells, whose blurry immensity is framed in a series of shots as the man sings grandly. After a set of interior images, the

7 Alexandra Pechman, "Leap of Faith." *Artforum*, 16 August 2016.

8 Gorbman, "Finding a Voice," 46.

film transitions to show an unpeopled landscape. In the same way, Rancière theorises the grand historical narratives of Jules Michelet as the "geographicisation" or "territorialisation" of the past, having the effect of "rendering [history] indiscernible from its place."[9] Similarly, here, history melts into the scenography on a beach in Normandy, where an old German bunker offers a readymade canvas for JR's antics. JR claims to have 'discovered' this bunker, a fantasy corrected by Varda's conversation with the local mayor, who explains that the bunker was knocked down in 1995 due to eroding cliffs. Despite Varda's intriguing suggestions (a nude of Guy Bourdin, or the crumpled corpse of a goat), JR selects an image that reflects his practice of personalising the landscape in the most anodyne way possible. The bunker's indelible evocation of war is unmentioned. Unassimilated, history is treated as an ephemeral image, washed away by the tide or blown away by the wind. The image pasted on the bunker disappears overnight, as if the sea and wind were taking their vengeance on the paper-thin plot of the film.

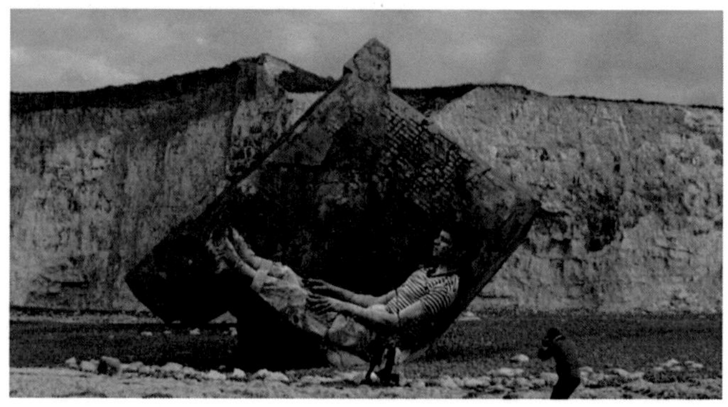

9 Jacques Rancière, *The Names of History: On the Poetics of Knowledge*, trans. Hassan Melehy (Minnesota University Press, 1994), 73.

The film propounds JR's sentimental approach to the image. The style and effect of his installations are reminiscent of a primary school art project, designed to elicit an affectionate attachment to place, less through aesthetic interest and more through personal connection. Such personal connection, however, is established by the abstraction of any content from the person; JR's images fixate on an abstracted human figure, rendered to adorn and anthropomorphise a building or surface, so as to create the sensation of encounter. Less an artist than a manager of aestheticised encounters, JR flirts with high-school girls, bestowing them with selfies and suggestive baguettes. These encounters ingratiate JR with the audience as a figure of desire. The overall effect is to render each personality-ridden scene a public relations exercise for JR.

This exercise constitutes the strongest current in *Visages Villages*, and plays out in the dynamic between JR and Varda. JR's condescension towards Varda's age and frailty reflects his usurpation of her authority over the image. He photographs her feet, from the bottom, in a dull, cold light suggestive of a mortuary, as if he were performing a forensic analysis. In scenes of image-making, JR intrudes on Varda's framing and direction. These moments suggest that JR is ushering out Varda's filmic authority and supplanting it with his own. In the very promotion of the film, JR carried around a cutout of Varda, meeting Hollywood celebrities and exploiting her image and identity as a pioneering female filmmaker to advance his own status. Varda's connection to *nouvelle vague* icons like Jean-Luc Godard offers JR an artistic credibility he clearly lacks. Motivated by little more than JR's Godard-esque gimmick of wearing sunglasses, they recreate the Louvre sequence from *Bande à part* (*Band of Outsiders*, 1964), competing to best that film's protagonists' time running through the galleries, with Varda consigned to a wheelchair. In a structurally disparate film, the conceit of chance associations has its charm.

However, it also renounces the sense of artistic direction or intention that had previously grounded Varda's imaginative associations. As Pechman suggests of JR's installations in Rio, his images are "not unlike a mirage propped over the real thing."[10]

In the concluding sequence of the film, Varda succumbs to JR's efforts to insinuate himself with the *nouvelle vague*'s central figure, Godard. Travelling to Godard's Swiss home, they are rebuffed by a closed door and a brusque note. In consoling Varda for her disappointment and sense of insult, JR suggests that Godard perhaps intended to contribute a "structural challenge" to their film. This interpretation falls flat, since the film's structure has been transparently thin. The closed door might, instead, symbolise the closure of an episode in film history, defined by a certain privileging of the image, or perhaps Varda's exclusion from the male-dominated *nouvelle vague*. One further interpretation is suggested by Godard's reference to Varda's *Du côté de la côte*, inserting a layer of irony and refusing to participate in what would be a sentimental conclusion to a film project he does not endorse.

JR refocuses the 'narrative' on himself in the melancholic aftermath of this failed encounter, which constitutes the dénouement of the film. He guides Varda to a seat beside a lake, where we listen in on their conversation from behind. Having effectively assimilated himself to the image of Godard through little more than his sunglasses, JR substitutes for the elusive icon by revealing his eyes to Varda. Not only does this gesture require JR's identification with Godard; it also aims to recuperate the film from Varda's disappointment with a triumphant but private revelation. Since the recuperation cannot match in stature Godard's absence, he becomes a haunting presence, threatening to overshadow Varda's own

10 Pechman, "Leap of Faith."

achievements. Instead of defending her resistance to assimilation within the *nouvelle vague*, or celebrating her, as Richard Neupert does, as a precursor and condition for the *nouvelle vague* ("grandmother," suggests Sheila Heti in an interview in *The Believer*; "ancestor," insists Varda in response), the viewer is left with JR's blurry face, compounding the emphasis on Varda's failing sight.[11] The image replaces the well-earned artistic link between Varda and Godard with a private and sentimental link between Varda and JR, and cheap artistic allusion.

As JR's personality supplants the historical development of a film aesthetic, the image's social currency supplants and assimilates its aesthetic quality. The film more broadly assimilates villagers to its project of urban gentrification, and turns deindustrialisation into the occasion for traversing the picturesque countryside in imitation of a tourism promotion. It treats historical debris as a decorative landscape. The film's technical derivativeness, sunny charm, and saccharine sentimentality serve the transmission of cultural credentials from the *nouvelle vague*. By sad contrast with Varda's larger body of work, *Visages Villages* transmutes industrial landscapes into conflictless advertisements for the French economy, people into placid, untroubled landscapes, and innovative aesthetic techniques into tropes to be re-adopted by commercial art. The film—and JR—may trade on Varda's artistic reputation, but its images do not reflect it.

11 "An Interview with Agnès Varda," interview by Sheila Heti, *The Believer*, October 1, 2009.

Michelle Huang

201 Minutes at the Capitol Theatre, 113 Swanston Street, Melbourne VIC 3000: *Jeanne Dielman, 23 quai du Commerce, 1080 Bruxelles* (1975)

At 23 Quai du Commerce, (now) 1000 Bruxelles, a plaque sits below the gold-coloured number 23, the oxide having eaten it with time, and reads: "C'est ici que Chantal Akerman a tourné son film en 1975." Then, in Dutch: "Hier heeft Chantal Akerman in 1975 haar film opgenomen." *"This is where Chantal Akerman shot her film in 1975."*

***

In 2022, the European Film Academy deemed this apartment block, named in the title of Chantal Akerman's 1975 film *Jeanne Dielman, 23 quai du Commerce, 1080 Bruxelles*, one of "35 Treasures of Film Culture," honouring its significance in European film history in an effort to preserve it for future generations.[1] Akerman's film is no stranger to this process of canonisation, especially in recent years, but such accolades have not been met with universal approval. The naming of *Jeanne Dielman* as the "Greatest Film of All Time" (according to the *Sight and Sound* 2022 critics' poll) incited uproar from some quarters. American filmmaker Paul Schrader

1 "Treasures of European Film Culture," European Film Academy, published November 2022.

complained on Facebook of a "politically correct rejiggering" of the *Sight and Sound* poll's once "reliable if somewhat incremental measure of critical consensus and priorities."[2] There is a certain irony to Schrader's complaint: as the first film by a woman to reach the top ten over the seventy-year history of the list, is the film's nomination not evidence enough of our times' progressive "critical consensus and priorities?" The *Sight and Sound* poll is a beloved resource for many scholars, filmmakers, critics, and cinephiles, but these attempts to condemn its alleged "distorted woke reappraisal" of the canon may also have drawn a wider audience of cinemagoers to decide for themselves. What's for sure is that this poll, and the discussion it has inspired, have led to more opportunities than ever to see Akerman's film on the big screen. I made my way to one of these screenings, at Melbourne's Capitol Theatre, in April 2023.

The three hours and twenty-one minutes of *Jeanne Dielman* are a meditation on ritual. Viewers dedicate 201 minutes of their lives to three days of mundanity with Jeanne, a widowed Belgian housewife and mother. The habits of her life stain the screen. The audience begins to anticipate her actions, while those moments of peculiarity which break the habits we've become used to make us jump with excitement. It is as though the fictional status of the film disintegrates with its run time. After the first hour, the repetition of action and camera angles starts to resemble surveillance footage of a lonely woman doing her daily chores of cooking, cleaning, and caring for her son—all until her routine falls apart. We viewers become habituated to the pace of her life. Each time Jeanne switches off the light, drops cash into a ceramic bowl, boils water, or sets up her son's bed, Akerman's trademark melancholic humour permeates the screen. You cannot help but laugh at the

2 Paul Schrader (@paul.schrader.900), Facebook, December 2, 2022.

performance of some of her actions, like knitting after dinner for less than a minute just for the sake of the ritual. Or there were the chuckles and scoffs from some in the audience when, after Jeanne neglects to switch on the radio as usual, her son demands she fulfil this task which he could easily carry out himself. This son, assuming the role of the male dependent, also expects Jeanne to carry on performing these habitual actions. Perhaps you had a similarly infuriated reaction to the friend I sat with at the Capitol, who turned to me with an exasperated sigh: "*Get up and help your mum!*"

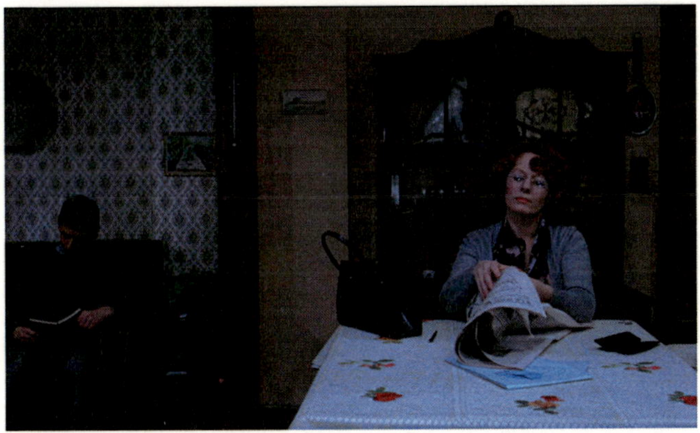

As a relative novice to the seventh art, the classification "slow cinema" that often arises in discussions of *Jeanne Dielman* made the film seem daunting and unapproachable to me. So I was gladly motivated to overcome this fear by the "Greatest Film of All Time" label Akerman's film received. A haunting sentiment looms over my lack of experience; a readiness for the consumption of this "genre" to transform my state of mind. Tonight, the slowness forces confrontation: a reluctance to walk away despite my—and everyone else's—endless shifting in the sterile Capitol seats. Inexperience leaves me with no choice but to continue out of sheer spite and fervent curiosity. Bluntly put, it would be hard to call the viewing experience enjoyable; it goes through stages that are equally painful, frustrating, and tedious.

But am I unique in having this experience, tonight at the Capitol? Being surrounded, I often catch myself watching these voyeurs as they watch Jeanne. This double act of watching amuses me, the restless aisles in my periphery affording no moment of silence. With the incessant traversal, the experience feels like a museum video installation rather than a screening—a format Akerman would work in at a later point in her career. Akerman invites spectators to cast their gaze onto Jeanne's body, allowing the audience to form their own interactions with the images unfolding before them. Some devote their attention for the full three hours and twenty-one minutes, while others grow fatigued by this art of surveillance, take their bags, and leave after a title card announces the "fin du premier jour" ("end of the first day"). Some exit the screening to stretch their legs, or use the bathrooms, or purchase refreshments. Maybe these audience reactions at the Capitol could be seen as a microcosm of the larger tendency to ignore women's labour, which Akerman has rendered visible. After all, life goes on (even today) behind the door of 23 Quai du Commerce, and behind so many doors in the streets we walk on every day. Is it boredom that has prompted me to question my spectatorship and to study this audience in relation to the film itself? Yet, if it is also boredom that provokes some to leave the cinema, perhaps this is an effect of the active participation asked for by Akerman's film. As Chiara Quaranta posits, with reference to Martin Heidegger, "profound boredom" is a strand of boredom which provides the necessary conditions for philosophising, and hence an aesthetic mode with the "potential to un-conceal ways we understand and interact with moving images."[3] A viewer may choose to accept or oppose this mood in their spectatorship, but at the Capitol tonight, I'm finding that being deliberately suspended in this state results in a new awareness. *Jeanne Dielman* and my conscious act of viewing—of both the film and the audience—will remain as an infrangible experience in my memory.

Spending three days with Jeanne seems to render time meaningless, yet time is the very heart of the film. Perhaps for Jeanne, and in watching her, we experience "time as entropy, as irreversibility."[4] It is the inevitable condition of inviting Akerman to experiment on viewers through her experimentations. Akerman plays with space and time, sound and silence, people and objects. She manipulates cinematic grammar, forcing you to expect something, and readily taking it away. This language pronounces anticipation by forcing our "boredom to remain awake."[5] It is a language that relentlessly nudges viewers, gently but firmly, to remind us of what we often forget: that women have always been there, and that there is a human figure behind the chores that provide for domestic survival. We stare intently upon this preprogrammed body of labour, intruding upon Jeanne's most intimate moments. This experience is hallucinatory—uncanny, even. You are absorbed by the soft teals and mustard tones on the screen, fully participating, yet fully gazing. You are absorbed by this elusive and shapeless space; almost real, almost a dream. The visual pleasure of the images seduces the spectators, but we are given an active choice in how we participate in this voyeurism: to ponder, to philosophise, to gaze, or to leave. I want

3 Chiara Quaranta, "A Cinema of Boredom: Heidegger, Cinematic Time and Spectatorship," *Film-Philosophy* 24, no. 1 (2020): 6.

4 Thierry de Duve, "Les Trois Horloges," in *Chantal Akerman*, Cahier 1, ed. Jaqueline Aubenas (Atelier des Arts, 1982), 89.

5 Quaranta, "A Cinema of Boredom," 6.

to understand Jeanne, but at the same time I feel at a great distance from her, like there is something that repels me, that tells me it would be easier to just turn away. I'm bored, but I'm so intrigued. I hate it, but I love it. I'm confused, but I get it. The dichotomies of these emotions are perturbingly satisfying. Of course, I don't—I can't—look away.

As Jeanne forgets the lid of her ceramic bowl and leaves a light on in another room, the tensions of the first two days collectively simmer until they reach the emotional break that concludes the third day and ends the film. But Akerman does not treat this break as a descent into madness, nor as hysteria, but approaches it with bone-chilling empathy. An easily forgotten moment during the third and final day still lingers in my mind: Jeanne sitting in an armchair, only breathing, waiting for time to pass. The mid shot encompasses the armchair and Jeanne's body, centred in its entirety, unobstructed by the kitchen bench, dining table or dressing table, as it often is. She is yearning for something she will never express, and which the audience will therefore never know. This view we have of her is imbued with melancholy, and with an intimacy that startles me. The surveillance-like distance is momentarily broken; suddenly, I feel like I am seeing Jeanne anew, and I find myself recalling the title of the film over and over: *Jeanne Dielman, 23 quai du Commerce, 1080 Bruxelles.* An audience's first encounter with the film is this title, this name and address. On the one hand, we might find something cold and impersonal in the title's flatness and length, situating Jeanne merely as the occupant of one household among untold others. But the specification of her address also humanises Jeanne, locating and identifying her. We step into the domestic space of one woman's life, among hundreds and thousands and millions in Brussels and beyond, bringing the forgotten everyday to visibility and recognition. Seeing what was once unseen is indelible.

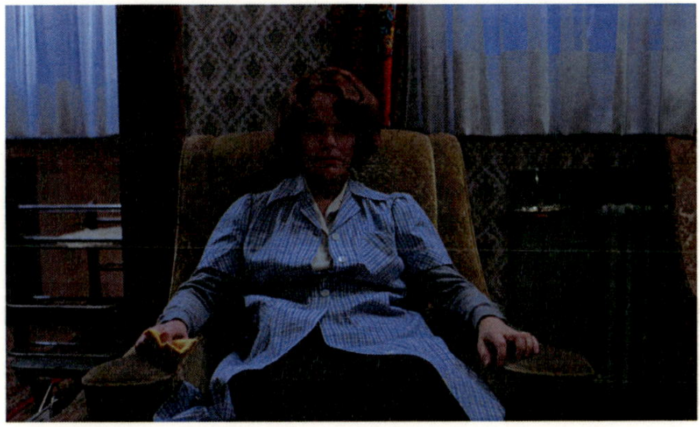

Finishing the film makes me want to immediately rewatch it; or perhaps, I never want it to end. I want to spend weeks or months more with Jeanne. *Jeanne Dielman* gives me the feeling I chase with every film I watch: the feeling of living, of always thinking about something, of holding on forever and ever. The most memorable cinematic experiences are those that inspire new emotions within me: the ones that take my breath away; the ones that make it hard to look upon the visage of people on the street outside of the cinema's darkened room. Maybe this is the best response to Schrader et al.: if a young film student from the other side of the world is occasionally reminded of the banal daily routine of a fictitious Belgian woman, even several months after having seen it, is that not ample proof that its renewed recognition has been worthwhile? The "Greatest Film of All Time" blurs "the boundary between those who act and those who look; between individuals and members of a collective body."[6] Liminal yet communal, each screening of *Jeanne Dielman* fuses the screen and the cinema

6 Jacques Rancière, *The Emancipated Spectator*, trans. Gregory Elliott (Verso, 2011), 18.

space, auteur and audience. Perhaps, if you look close enough, you will find elation filling Jeanne's idle hallways, opening the door to the boredom wishing to tell us something.

Index of Films Cited

À nos amours (Maurice Pialat, 1983): 21–29

Acéphale (Patrick Deval, 1968): 45–52

Actua 1 (Philippe Garrel, 1968): 44

Afrique sur Seine (Paulin Soumanou Vieyra, 1955): 42

L'Amour fou (Jacques Rivette, 1969): 2, 3, 8, 9, 31–43, 83, 84

L'Argent de poche (*Small Change*, François Truffaut, 1976): 55

L'Aventure c'est L'Aventure (Claude Lelouch, 1972): 40

Bande à part (*Band of Outsiders*, Jean-Luc Godard, 1964): 97

Le Beau Serge (Claude Chabrol, 1958): 3

The Big Country (William Wyler, 1958): 14

Céline et Julie vont en bateau (*Celine and Julie Go Boating*, Jacques Rivette, 1974): 12, 13, 18

Un chien andalou (Luis Buñuel and Salvador Dali, 1929): 91

Chronique d'un été (*Chronicle of a Summer*, Edgar Morin and Jean Rouch, 1961): 42

Closed Vision (Marc'o, 1954): 71

Daguerréotypes (Agnès Varda, 1975): 89, 91

Du côté de la côte (*Along the Coast*, Agnès Varda, 1958): 87, 89, 92, 95, 98

Deux fois (Jackie Raynal, 1968): 47

L'Enfant sauvage (*The Wild Child*, François Truffaut, 1970): 53–67

Les Enfants du Paradis (Marcel Carné, 1945): 13

Les Glaneurs et la glaneuse (*The Gleaners and I*, Agnès Varda, 2000): 89, 93, 94

Héraclite l'obscur (Patrick Deval, 1967): 45

Les Idoles (Marc'o, 1968): 69–86

Jeanne Dielman, 23 Quai du Commerce, 1080 Bruxelles (Chantal Akerman, 1975): 2, 3, 8, 101–8

Jules et Jim (François Truffaut, 1961): 7, 55

Lonely Boy (Wolf Koenig and Roman Kroitor, 1962): 80

La Maman et la putain (*The Mother and the Whore*, Jean Eustache, 1973): 2, 3, 7, 8, 69, 84, 85

The Long Good Friday (John Mackenzie, 1980): 19

Masculin féminin (Jean-Luc Godard, 1966): 5–7, 84

La Noire de . . . (*Black Girl*, Ousmane Sembène, 1966): 42

L'Œil humain (*The Human Eye*, Xavier Giannoli, 1999): 28, 29

Out 1 (Jacques Rivette, 1971): 11

Paris nous appartient (*Paris Belongs to Us*, Jacques Rivette, 1959): 33

Persona (Ingmar Bergman, 1966): 49

Pink Floyd: The Wall (Alan Parker, 1982): 84

La Piscine (Jacques Deray, 1969): 40

La Pointe Courte (Agnès Varda, 1955): 3

Le Pont du Nord (Jacques Rivette, 1981): 11–19

Purple Rain (Albert Magnoli, 1984): 84

Les Quatre Cents Coups (*The 400 Blows*, François Truffaut, 1959): 7, 60, 61, 76

La Religieuse (*The Nun*, Jacques Rivette, 1966): 33

Ô saisons, ô châteaux (Agnès Varda, 1958): 95

Sans toit ni loi (*Vagabond*, Agnès Varda, 1985): 89

Sauve qui peut (la vie) (Jean-Luc Godard, 1980): 9

Scénario de Sauve qui peut (la vie) (Jean-Luc Godard, 1979): 9–10

Soleil Ô (Med Hondo, 1967): 42

Tommy (Ken Russell, 1975): 84

Traité de bavé et d'éternité (*Treatise on Venom And Eternity*, Isidore Isou, 1951): 71

L'une chante, l'autre pas (*One Sings, the Other Doesn't*, Agnès Varda, 1977): 89, 92

Velvet Goldmine (Todd Haynes, 1998): 84

Visages Villages (JR and Agnès Varda, 2017): 10, 87–99

Zoé bonne (Patrick Deval and Christian Ledoux, 1966): 45

Acknowledgments

Thanks to everyone who was involved in the French Film Club at the University of Melbourne, including (in addition to all of the authors in this collection) Alicia Byrnes, Louise Cain, Jon Dale, Tess Do, Cristóbal Escobar, Emma Fajgenbaum, Simon Killen, Damien Laing, Hazel Lanyon, Darcy Lazarus, Janice Loreck, Leah Jing McIntosh, Sally Ann McIntyre, Chris Pullin, Kelvin Skewes, Katia Tulyakova, Campbell Walker, Mark Wilson, and Damon Young. That experiment, and the community we formed through it, remains important to all of us, and we hope to find ways of renewing it into the future, starting with this book.

Many thanks also to Rosa Gaetano, and to Giles Fielke and the team at Index.